# INTO THE SHADOWS

## A JOURNEY INTO PARANORMAL INVESTIGATION

ALLISON ROBINS

Copyright © 2022 by Allison Robins

All rights reserved.

No part of this book may be reproduced in any form or by any electronic or mechanical means, including information storage and retrieval systems, without written permission from the author, except for the use of brief quotations in a book review.

# Contents

| | |
|---|---|
| Prologue | 1 |
| 1. A French Haunting<br>*The Start of My Paranormal Journey* | 5 |
| 2. Paranormal Investigating | 17 |
| 3. Family Visits & Haunted Writing Desks<br>*My Paranormal Experiences...* | 25 |
| 4. Time, Superstition & The Paranormal<br>*Just My Musings...* | 31 |
| 5. The Ghost Child & The 'Thing'<br>*My Paranormal Experiences...* | 37 |
| 6. So, You Think You'd Like To Be A Paranormal Investigator? | 47 |
| 7. The Bird And The Butterfly<br>*My Paranormal Experiences...* | 57 |
| 8. The Pitfalls - Tales Of The Unexpected<br>*(The Hazards of Being a Paranormal Investigator)* | 69 |
| 9. Psychics & Mediums<br>*The Opening up of a Whole New World...* | 77 |
| 10. It's All About The Energy<br>*Some More of my Musings...* | 89 |
| 11. Home Again ...In Cornwall<br>*My Paranormal Experiences...* | 99 |
| 12. So... You Still Want To Investigate? | 109 |
| 13. Footsteps<br>*My Paranormal Experiences...* | 117 |
| 14. Equipment<br>*The Paranormal Technological Boom...* | 125 |
| 15. The Shadow Man<br>*My Paranormal Experiences...* | 141 |
| 16. Frequency<br>*Yet More Musings...* | 151 |

17. Apports - Little Presents From Beyond — 161
*My Paranormal Experiences...*

18. Staying Safe In Our Paranormal World — 169
*More of Those Pesky Hazards...*

19. The Attic Children — 179
*My Paranormal Experiences...*

20. To Ouija Or Not To Ouija? — 191
*That, is the Question...*

21. Table Tipping — 201
*My Paranormal Experiences...*

22. Past Lives — 207
*Yes, I mused again!*

23. Paranormal Experiments — 217
*Having Fun with Spirit...*

24. The Typical Investigation — 225

25. The Ouija Board & Alice — 237
*My Paranormal Experiences...*

26. Our Natural State Of Being — 245
*Yes, I Have Thought Some More...*

27. A Sense Of Place — 251
*What Makes a Place Haunted?...*

28. When Investigations Go Wrong — 261

29. Back To The Shadows — 269
*My Paranormal Experiences...*

Epilogue — 283

About the Author — 287

# Prologue

*Seeing is believing*, the old adage goes – and I, at last, have seen.

At approximately 2:15 am on a cold March morning, I was finally to experience that holy grail of the paranormal world – *the full apparition*.

Striding purposefully into the cell flanked 'Long Room' at the infamous Bodmin Jail, he (for it most certainly was a 'he') was in perfect silhouette. Softly backlit by the pale light of our base room, he was moving fast. Very fast. He crossed in front of the static infrared camera – set up in the hope of catching just such an occurrence – and as he reached the furthest, darkest corner of the room, he simply *ceased to be*.

What did I feel about this occurrence? Was I scared? Joyous? – *Excited?*

No. Truth be told, I was just bewildered. So confident was I that I had been watching a *real* man enter the room, that it simply never crossed my mind that I had actually just seen a spirit. Even after he'd disappeared – I was left trying to rationalise what I had just witnessed.

When, at last, the investigator in me kicked in, I hurried to the base room to where I knew I would find the team poring over the monitors.

'Play it back. Something has just walked right in front of the camera.'

'I would...' came the weary response, 'If only that *something* hadn't turned off the record button.'

And that's what it's like to investigate the paranormal.

The endless quest for proof that we know, deep down, we're never going to get. At least – none that would satisfy everyone, anyway.

You know what they say, 'for the believer, no proof is necessary – but for the non-believer, no proof is possible.'

So why bother?

The answer to that is simple. It's because once you've tried it and got a little bit of response in the form of tapping, footsteps or a disembodied voice or three, then it's already too late – you're hooked!

Suddenly life becomes all about those cold, uncomfortable hours that you spend sitting in some horrid, dark, spider-infested hovel – and worse still, you will pay through the nose for the privilege.

For me, the justification comes from getting proof that I can believe. I don't worry too much about what other people think – after all, they weren't there. They didn't feel the sudden chill in the air – or that amazing sense of presence that literally makes your hair stand on end.

I'm sure every paranormal investigator has their own personal word for that feeling. Mine, is *the buzz*. It's like the very air around you is *alive* with static, and you know – you just *know*, that a spirit is close.

So how did my journey into the paranormal begin?

Well, it started in a hot sunny country, and about as far away from anything 'spooky' as you could possibly imagine – the rugged beauty of Southwest France, way down – towards the Spanish border.

## Chapter 1
# A French Haunting
The Start of My Paranormal Journey

The next time you settle down with a travel brochure to book a gîte in the tranquil beauty of rural France, spare a thought, will you, towards the history of the place – it just might not be as serene as it first appears.

In the spring of 2002, tired of the rat race that was England, I set off – determined to build a new life for me and my family. The search for that idyllic new home, eventually beckoning me to an ancient hilltop village located in the upper regions of the Hautes-Pyrénées.

I knew I wanted the house the moment I set eyes on it. A rambling L-shaped Gascon farmhouse with a forlorn, faded grandeur. Built in 1779, and virtually derelict now. Buried, as it was, under shoulder-high weeds and shrouded in a thick blanket of cobwebs – it was just crying out to be loved – to be brought back to life! The decider though, the real clincher – was its abundance of outbuildings. Here, at last, was the potential to create our very own *dreamed-of* gîte.

Near bursting with excitement and enthusiasm, we shook on the deal, signed on the *many* dotted lines, and moved in – launching ourselves into the task of creating a home from that long-neglected jewel.

There was electricity and plumbing to be installed, a kitchen to fit and bedrooms to be formed from those empty, dust-covered attics. So much to do – but the renovations had barely begun, when we started to notice odd little occurrences.

Every evening at roughly the same time, there would be a single hard tap on the glass of the back window of the living room – even when the external wooden shutters were closed.

At first, we reasoned that it must have been a bird – too used to the window being open and expecting to still be able to fly through. But quite honestly, it would need to have been the dumbest bird ever!

Weeks went by – then months, and still it continued (although obviously, we'd discounted the bird idea by then). We never did catch sight of what was causing it, though – and it never stopped.

Amongst other little oddities – the door to my daughter's room would often slowly swing open during the night, even though the latch had been firmly closed. There were times that her television (not remote-controlled) would turn itself on, and the many occasions that she'd lie awake in the night, listening intently to the sounds of movement within her room.

Needless to say, she soon switched bedrooms – but it didn't help. Whatever it was, soon followed to her new room.

Worth also noting at this point – was on the several occasions that my husband slept in that room – he'd take to jamming a chair under the handle to prevent the door from opening. Something it never did during the day, or if the room was unoccupied.

It's amazing what you get used to, eh?

Now that restoration of the main house was finally finished, I pushed all thoughts of ghosts to the back of my mind – and with an eye to securing our future, cracked on. Turning my attention now, to the conversion of one of the smaller connecting barns.

It was time to create that gorgeous little holiday home first envisaged all those months ago. Our French adventure would be so much easier if we could achieve a small, regular rental income.

Centuries of dust and grime were cleared as we worked on replacing the woodworm-ridden flooring and rotten first-floor beams – and it was not without its drama, as my husband was soon to find out.

Whilst standing at the top of the original rickety staircase and pondering the best way to dismantle it, suddenly, it did the job for him – dumping him unceremoniously in a cloud of dust, dirt, and powdered wood. Luckily, the only thing wounded that day was his pride, as the event became the subject of many a light-hearted jibe within the family.

Anyway, internal walls went up, the bathroom and kitchen were fitted and then came the fun part – decoration. Visits to the local brocante yielded antique furniture, lighting, and soft furnishings – and with work on the gîte now complete, we were excitedly awaiting the arrival of our first paying guests. Little did we suspect, at this point, that the cottage was essentially already occupied.

It slowly became apparent, that our guests just weren't comfortable sleeping in the twin room – the back bedroom. Although a lovely cosy room by day, it seemed to take on a different persona at nightfall.

Visitors recounted a sudden dramatic cold (which, in the height of a French summer, is notable indeed) that would linger a few minutes before disappearing just as rapidly.

There would be taps and heavy knocking noises, the sound of footsteps on the stairs, and one guest even divulged being awakened by something temporarily pinning them to the bed!

An American family en route to Italy, were particularly affected whilst holidaying with us. The ten-year-old son had simply refused to sleep in that room, insisting on joining his mother in the front double. Of more interest to me, though, was discovering that the father had, likewise, declined to sleep in the back bedroom. He'd been taking the bedding each night and making up a bed on the sofa instead.

Obviously, we never mentioned the risk of possible ghostly activity to our guests, prior to their stay. For one thing – we didn't want them turning about and taking off again! No – we kept quiet. Just taking note of a chance embarrassed comment, or listening carefully to what they willingly reported.

In the main house, the light activity continued sporadically – causing us no real distress, but frequently piquing my interest. It was the start of the whole paranormal tv age – and yes, I'm prepared to admit, it caught my attention. Inspiring me to start a bit of light investigation of my own.

I purchased my first digital recorder, an Olympus DM-670, and began leaving it just about anywhere, to see what activity I could catch – including one overnight session in the neighbouring château, an historic 18th-century manor house.

It was a spooky old place, for sure – one that gave off strange vibes. You always felt somehow – watched. And if truth be told, I was a little on edge as I'd crept in alone to position the recorder in the lower grand salon. But oh, how you'd have enjoyed seeing me skedaddling out of there.

And talking of skedaddling – I must confess to scaring my daughter and her best friend half to death, whilst they were there a few days later. They'd been hired to do a clean-through prior to the arrival of visitors, and the chance for a bit of extra pocket money was never to be turned down.

Needing to speak to her about something or other – I entered the château via the barn and had stopped by the stairs to listen. The upper storey linked directly with the landing of the main house, although the connecting door was always locked.

I could hear the girls – happily chatting as they toiled away in the hallway beyond, without an apparent care in the world. Well, the devil took hold of me that day, and I couldn't resist.

Creeping silently up to the door, I grasped the doorknob and without stopping to think of the consequences, rattled it violently, twisting it back and forth.

The result was instantaneous and hilarious *(well, for me, anyway)*. Two terrified teenagers simultaneously screamed, threw down the brush and mop and took off at a rate of knots – feet clattering noisily on the stairs.

What made it all the funnier though, was that they had run in the wrong direction. They'd stranded themselves on a bedroom balcony – unable to proceed further and powerless to pluck up the courage needed to re-enter the house and exit the right way, down the main stairs. That is – until they'd finally calmed down enough to hear my laughter.

Oh, I am a BAAAAAD mother!

So, after all that, the results of the château recording turned out to be nondescript. But I persevered, and luckily enough *(is this actually lucky? – some would say not)*, the recordings taken in my own place, turned out to be much better. Indeed, some were *really* odd.

Over the course of the following few weeks, I caught the sounds of approaching footsteps and strange, muffled whisperings and a weird groan. The one that really freaked out the kids, though *(should I still be calling teenagers that?)*, was one of my better captures. I'd placed the recorder on a cross beam on the upstairs landing, and had gone for a brief walk, leaving no one present in the house.

When the kids *(sorry – habit!)* had asked me to play it for their friends to see what they would make of it, things quickly became emotional. Everyone present that day unanimously agreed on what they'd heard – and it had come in the perfectly accented dialect of the region. It was an unmistakable 'Je suis là' *(I am here!)*

*Very* freaky!

Spooked now, it had literally brought tears to their eyes.

Even freakier for me though, was the later capture of what appeared to be one half of a conversation from a distant part of the house.

The recording was of a woman, talking softly and seemingly in French – although I couldn't make out any of the words. She would speak, and then there would be a pause – just silence on the recorder *(had she been listening, maybe?)*, before talking once again. It was not unlike hearing someone on a phone.

I was excited to share this evidence with family and friends, but was dismayed and disheartened when they all just shook their heads, saying, 'That's just you talking, isn't it?'

Of course, I assured them that it wasn't.

Yes, I was present. But I had remained silent throughout.

But the doubt was there now, wasn't it?

So, what was happening? Was spirit mimicking my voice? I know now that they can, and do – but at that time, I knew little of these things – except that it was frustrating as hell not to be believed.

Years have now gone by – my family has grown, and my daughter is living in the gîte. She was never to be totally alone there though, at least, not in the spiritual sense.

All too often, she would hear those footsteps – coming up the stairs to cross the floor behind the settee, only to glance back and find that it wasn't me, or indeed – *anyone*. Sometimes, she would phone me in the night, after hearing it again – just for comfort. But I give her full credit – she stayed put.

A few short months later, however, it was to be *my* turn to be put to the test. And it would happen while my husband and son were away from home, visiting family in England.

Alone in the house, I retired to bed as usual and had fallen asleep readily enough. It was in the early hours, though, and still full dark, that I was jerked into instant wakefulness.

Was that the sound of footsteps? *On the stairs*?

I glanced at the clock, 03:07.

The sound was getting louder now, closer – *just outside my room!* Then, for a moment at least, everything stopped, and a heavy silence hung over the house.

Staring intently at the door and barely daring to breathe, I listened, wide-eyed, as a series of weird scraping, dragging noises, began filtering through from the hallway beyond.

There was a squeal of tortured wood, as something was

hauled across the floor. *The chest, maybe?* – surely the only thing out there heavy enough to make that much noise. A strange scuffling followed, and then finally, *thankfully*, the footsteps retreated back down the stairs and faded away.

The fact that it could have been a burglar simply never crossed my mind – I just *knew* it wasn't. The air was, somehow, *charged*.

Well, I didn't sleep a wink for the rest of that night, and in the dim light of dawn, I poked my head out the door. Nothing had moved. Nothing had changed.

What had made that dragging noise? I had no idea. The chest hadn't moved – and neither had the chair, the only other piece of furniture on the landing.


So, that was how it happened, and this time, it was me that had the activity – not my daughter and not our guests.

I had heard the footsteps. It had happened to ME!


Well, that was the start of my obsession with the paranormal. It had always been a strong interest, but now it exploded into my life. One way or another – I just *knew* that I was going to investigate the paranormal.

To follow that dream, I sold my beautiful French

farmhouse – my home for over ten years. I returned to Cornwall... and the rest, as they say, is history.

So – do the new owners think the place is haunted?

I would hazard a guess that by *now*, they do.

Are they bothered? I don't know – you'd have to ask them. But for me, it was always just part of the charm of the place.

Chapter 2
# Paranormal Investigating

What are *your* thoughts on Paranormal Investigators?

Are we crackpots *(be gentle with me here, please)* deserving of nothing more than a pat on the head and a knowing smile, or are we simply the coolest people ever? I'd like to think we come somewhere nearer the latter – but if I'm honest, I've met all too many that would fall squarely into the first category.

Yes, there are those who claim every speck of dust caught by the camera is an orb, or that spirits reside within the lens flare of a picture taken whilst pointing the camera into the Sun – but then who's to categorically say that they are wrong? After all, could not a spirit have manipulated them somehow, into taking that particular shot, at that precise time, with a view to creating that phenomenon?

And therein lies the problem. What, for one, is proof of phenomena, will disprove it for another.

Let's just take the example of EMF.

*Electromagnetic Fields* are areas of invisible energy, that are associated with light and the use of electrical power. You might hear it referred to as radiation, and it *is* radiation, but we're not talking about levels deserving of that well-known yellow and black trefoil symbol here, but just your basic background stuff.

There's a vast amount of supposed paranormal equipment sold today that is based solely upon the reading of EMF changes. But does a sudden spike registered on an EMF meter really mean that a spirit is present? Or could it just be that an unforeseen change in the natural electromagnetic field that constantly surrounds us, has caused the device to activate? Leading the inexperienced user to believe that a spirit is close, and maybe trigger them, in turn, to physically sense its presence.

It happens. We've all done it.

When people start to think about spooky things, they get jumpy, *right*?

Just the well-told recounting of a ghostly experience can be all it takes to trigger a physical response from its listener. They may actually start to *feel* that chill, complete with shudders, goosebumps... the lot.

Our body is an extraordinary tool. It reacts to the

(seen and unseen) world around us, in amazing ways – but it is controlled, for the most part, by the mind.

You need to stay objective when dealing with the paranormal. Ask yourself, 'Am I really feeling that, or am I permitting nerves or excitement get to me?'

Don't allow yourself to be led, by what other people say *they* are experiencing or feeling. View the evidence from all sides and make up your own mind.

Another bone of contention in the paranormal world is the presence of infrasound – soundwaves with a frequency below the threshold of normal human hearing.

Infrasound typically has a frequency of less than 20Hz, but it is only at the very lowest end of that range, way down below 5Hz, that it will become totally inaudible to most people.

Scientific studies have proven that when humans come into contact with infrasound, they may become panicky, anxious and sometimes even nauseous – which, as you can imagine, would also be grounds for suspecting possible paranormal activity.

Why does it cause this reaction? Well, I'm not a scientist, but it something to do with the vibration of energy. Everything around us, and I do mean *everything* – even that seemingly solid table you're sitting at – is constantly vibrating. The rate of vibration for individual items, including we humans, will vary though.

Now, if we were to come into contact with a

soundwave frequency that vibrates at a rate similar to ours (at or around 7.5Hz), it could cause an interference – a change to our fundamental state of being. That said, it's pretty straightforward to comprehend that, yes – infrasound will definitely affect us.

So – some will rightly say that undetected infrasound may cause feelings of presence, making you feel anxious, scared – or watched. Others, however, will claim that the very presence of infrasound itself, can attract paranormal activity – leading you to that very same feeling!

So, you see, it is neither possible to definitively prove, nor disprove the paranormal. It's something that you will just have to learn to accept and come to your own decision – your own happy medium.

Complicating a difficult conundrum still further, is the phenomenal rise in the popularity of paranormal programming on television, and barely a day goes by without some spooky offering or other.

Paranormal tv has so much to offer. It opens our world to us, allowing us to experience wonderful historic buildings and to learn about the plethora of hauntings reported there over the years. Places that, let's face it, most of us will never get the opportunity to see for ourselves in real life. But tv also has a lot to answer for, too.

A televised paranormal series has, by its very nature, a major conflict of interest. True paranormal investigation is, for the most part, very dull. It's cold, it's dark, and nothing is usually happening. This is obviously a huge no-no for television, and inevitably leads to the faking of evidence. How could it not?

No self-respecting tv producer will want to air a programme in which nothing is happening. They will push participants for a better facial reaction to that creak – or a replay of that door swinging open. And once you go down that route, then it's only a small jump to the creating of evidence in the first place – in order to craft a better finished product.

For me, *any* programme or person that receives significant money for their documented investigations, will need to be taken with a generous pinch of salt.

Enjoy the programme by all means. I still do *(well... some of them anyway)*. Revel in the chance to see extraordinary and beautiful places – take in the tales of ghosts from a bygone age, but don't believe all you see or are told. They are, after all, just a money-making exercise.

I think it fair to say that most paranormal investigators *(at least the ones I know)* undeniably spend the best part of their paranormal tv sessions shouting loudly and rudely at the telly! I mean – *what do they expect*?

It's hard not to, when the programme presenter doubles down, insisting that it *'must have been a ghost'* that just slammed that door – and that it had *'nothing whatsoever to do with the howling wind outside.'* Meh.

The vast majority of paranormal television programmes nowadays, tend to follow an all too predictable pattern.

The introduction to the chosen investigation site *(with a few B-roll shots thrown in, to set the scene – and cue the suitably spooky music, of course!)* An interview or three, with some of the people, said to be affected by the 'haunting'. A few hours of running around with a night vision camera and, finally, closure – during which they can pat themselves firmly on the back for having sent the spirit *'into the light'*, and thereby having saved the day.

Do I sound a bit jaded on the subject? Well – yes. I guess I am, a little.

I'm still hoping, waiting for someone to come up with something new – something exciting. I would love to see an extended, in-depth investigation. One where static cameras and recorders are left running over many weeks. Paranormal activity does not happen every day. Weeks and even months, can go by between occurrences.

I would certainly sit up and take notice if someone were to go to the trouble of producing evidence using these methods. But sadly, it will never happen, and here's why...

Filming over extended periods would require vast amounts of man hours, even if only to thoroughly review the footage for any potential evidence. And quite simply, time is money.

There are still plenty of occasions though, when something shown on the small screen manages to grab my attention. True, I might watch most, with one eye firmly on my phone – but show me something that I can't easily explain, and I'm instantly in the zone.

Yes, I can still enjoy a good bit of well-crafted paranormal tv – as long as there is no screaming!

I don't tolerate that – and it remains the one thing that, without fail, will have me instantly reaching for the off button. Come on! I mean, how would it even be possible to be that scared? And after so many years of investigating?

In all honesty though, throughout every investigation I have ever undertaken, no one has ever screamed. Well – not a proper one anyway – and not because of a ghost.

Spooky films though, are a whole other ball game for me.

Believe it or not, although I am quite at home walking through a known haunted location in the pitch-black, with nothing but a camera for protection, I bizarrely find myself unable to watch paranormal movies.

I just can't.

Oh, I know full well that it is all just acting. Just smoke and mirrors – and an awful lot of make-up, of course.

But honestly, they just scare me!

A fact that remains a constant cause of hilarity to others in my field. They just can't get their heads around how I can be so brave on the one hand, yet wimp out when it comes to mere films.

I can though, and I can give two valid reasons.

The first, is my recent discovery that movie makers of the horror and supernatural genre purposefully insert *infrasound* into their soundtrack – surreptitiously bringing on that sense of anxiety or unease in the viewer.

*Unbelievable...!* The cheeky b@$*@£d$.

And the second reason? Ah yes... the second is that in the real world, people don't get 'hacked up' by ghosts.

At least – not that I've come across, *yet*!

## Chapter 3
# Family Visits & Haunted Writing Desks

My Paranormal Experiences…

Having regaled you at some length with my ghostly experiences in France, I am now in the mood to share more. And there have been so many experiences over the years. So much to tell.

Truth be told, I now believe my first ever trip into this paranormal world of ours, was when I was just a small child, somewhere in the vicinity of just five years of age.

Snuggled cosily in the double bed that had lately been my grandparents', I had found my attention unexpectedly drawn towards a painting that had hung, seemingly forever, above the soot-blackened fireplace.

Ordinarily, it was a faded watercolour of a small, insignificant yacht, embattled by a raging sea – yet now, bizarrely, there was no such scene. In its place was the clear head and shoulders image of my grandmother, her body turned slightly away, her head angled towards me with eyes downcast.

As I watched, mildly terrified and clutching at the sheets, she lifted her head, looked straight at me, and gave me the loveliest of smiles. She didn't speak, she didn't move – it was just that wonderful, loving smile.

I have no recollection of anything happening after the bestowing of that beautiful smile. *Surely*, I couldn't have immediately fallen asleep? – Not after that?

I simply don't know – but can only imagine that I must have.

All I *do* know, is that it was now a bright sunny morning, and all was well with the world. The yacht was once more plunging through the waves, and there was no sign whatsoever that there had ever been anything else.

Of course, I mentioned none of this to my parents and came, soon enough, to write off the whole experience as just another dream – but these days, I trust I know better.

Why would I remember a mere dream, in such vivid detail?

I genuinely now believe that it was my grandmother – that she had been trying to show me just how much I was still loved – and for that, I am blessed indeed.

. . .

Thinking back, it was no great surprise that I should have had my first paranormal experience there, in *that* house. That quaint little two up, two down end of terrace that was home to my grandparents throughout their married life.

My dear grandad, to whom I was so very close, used to entertain me with all kinds of spine-chilling tales, and I loved him all the more for it.

'The Red Lady of Bodiam Castle', 'the faceless airman, crouched eternally in the corner of a long-deserted airfield...' oh, he had a ton of them.

But my favourite... my 'go to' story – was always the haunted writing desk and I would badger him about it until he gave in and would settle down to tell me the tale once again.

The desk in question was an $18^{th}$-century Georgian, drop-fronted writing bureau – filled with an exciting *(to my young mind anyway)* array of wonders – and it had stood in the corner of the tiny cottage living room.

Gifted to my grandad for long and loyal service, by the late owner of the village Manor, where he'd been Head Gardener for all those years – it had come complete with *all* its contents.

Prior to her untimely death, my dear grandmother had been ill – so *very* ill. She'd suffered greatly from rheumatoid arthritis, which had eventually resulted in the loss of one of her legs and caused her constant chronic pain in the other.

In the last years of her life, being unable now to mount the stairs to her bedroom, she'd taken, instead, to sleeping on a makeshift bed in the living room. And it was there, in that tiny yet cosy room, that the inexplicable occurrences that I want to tell you about were to take place.

Lying in her bed of a night, my gran would often struggle to sleep – and it wasn't just the pain that could bring on a restless night.

Time and again, she would heartily complain about being disturbed in the night – by the sound of someone sitting at *that* desk. About how she'd lie awake in the darkness, listening to shuffling noises, sighs, the little scratching sounds of pen on paper and the light scrape of the trinkets within being moved about.

Oh, how my grandad had light-heartedly teased her. He'd pooh-pooh her complaints and imply that she must have been dreaming – or if not, that her imagination had simply been running overtime – probably brought on by all those strong medications.

She, my gran, was adamant though – and as it turned out, was to finally get the last laugh.

My father, who had been away serving his two years conscription in the army, had been offered the living room to sleep in, when he temporarily returned home on leave.

The following morning, as the three of them were sat in the kitchen eating breakfast, he'd casually remarked, 'You know... I didn't get a wink of sleep last night. I kept thinking there was someone in the room with me – but every time I turned on the lights, there was no one there.'

'Hah!' said my gran, eyeing her husband triumphantly. 'I told you!'

Time has moved on *(too much time, for sure)*, and so has the desk, though always within the family.

A strange little addendum here is that my mother, many years ago, had submitted to having her palm read by a travelling gypsy woman, who was intent on selling her some 'lucky lavender'.

As she'd studied her palm, the gypsy had bizarrely remarked, 'That bit of furniture you have – the one with the spirit attachment – make sure you keep it in the family. It will bring you good luck.'

Well, we have since taken that advice to heart. My mother took it first, then handed it down to me, and I in turn, have handed it down to my daughter.

See – I *told* you she was brave, didn't I!

So, what now of that desk and the spirit within? Is it still active?

Sadly, no – not at this point in time anyway.

Whilst still in the possession of my mother, she had unfortunately taken it upon herself to clear out much of its contents. Personal journals, some watercolours that the ladies of the house had painted, and most notably, a monogrammed lace handkerchief. A dainty little thing that had been neatly folded and perfectly pressed into shape. It had been discovered tucked inside a tiny compartment, concealed at the back of a secret drawer – one that could only be released by the pressing of a hidden lever.

I have to wonder – could it have been the removal of these items that had caused the cessation of activity?

Sadly, I would have to say yes – *probably*. Although who knows what the future may bring?

Just maybe, the activity had been because of my gran. Perhaps it was an attempt at keeping her company in her time of need – to ease her into her next incarnation.

If so, in years to come, just *maybe*, it will start again.

I guess only time will tell.

Chapter 4

# Time, Superstition & The Paranormal

Just My Musings...


Time is a strange concept. An invisible barrier that separates us from all that has gone before.

Think about it... where you are right now! If time somehow didn't exist, if only for a moment, what would you see? A bleak workhouse corridor? A long-since demolished farmstead? Or maybe an open heathland, alive with grazing animals and the soft hum of insects?

What *is* time? I don't know – it's elusive. It seems to me though, to be flexible. Somehow ...*stretchy*.

Those wonderful excitement-filled days of our early childhood had seemed to go on forever. Long hot summers and endless days of exploration have turned instead, into a never-ending rolling over of day into night, night into day – that seems to be continually speeding up, hastening us towards our own old age.

Yet time, for most at least, will remain of vital importance.

'Mustn't be late.'

'Must get to bed by nine, if I'm going to be fresh for the morning.'

Or maybe – 'Must put the kettle on at eleven' for that much-anticipated cup of tea. I mean – obviously, the tea couldn't possibly taste the same, were it to be made at say, eleven-thirty for example.

Maybe, you'll find yourself in a situation where you're wishing your time away.

Counting down the weeks until you get to see your loved one again – or perhaps watching the clock; urging on that second hand, as it laboriously ticks off the remainder of your working day.

Time has become all too important in our hectic modern life, putting pressure on all of us to accomplish and conform.

Could that be why so many people have bestowed special meaning to certain times of the day – midnight and 3 am being but two common examples.

Could it be some sort of spiritual comfort blanket? Providing a sense of reassurance, of importance, for those seeking their place within the chaotic reality that is our world?

Others, however, will give much greater credence to

the sighting of certain repeated numbers – such as 11:11 or 3:33.

Commonly known as '*Angel Numbers*' – if you keep coming across recurring 1s in your day-to-day life, then it's considered to be a sign of a new beginning, a new chapter in your life – maybe the opening of new opportunities. Whereas recurring 3s could indicate that you need to get more inventive with your life... I don't know, maybe get arty – or write a book or something!

Others will see these repeated numbers as some kind of portent, a spiritual message, if you like, from beyond and will elevate their perceived importance until they hold ludicrous significance in their lives.

But are these numbers really significant? – when it comes to time, in particular?

Imagine for a moment, if you will, a big old analogue clock, reading 11:11. Think about the position of the hands. Now do the same for 3:33. It's the same scenario – all sense of significance is now completely lost.

As I ponder on time and its relationship with the paranormal, I begin to wonder... If time is flexible, could it maybe, '*bend*' – just a little? Enough, perhaps, to allow a glimpse of a figure from an earlier age? Could *that* explain some instances of apparitions from the past? There are undoubtedly many documented reports of people said to have experienced such an event.

Maybe, that's what had caused the activity from the writing desk? All those years ago. Could that have been some sort of time slip? Somehow allowing the sounds of a bygone age to seep through, to be heard by my grandmother – disturbing her nights and keeping her awake.

Could it...?

Maybe...?

What if...? My thoughts just lead to more and more questions.

While futilely contemplating the strange concept that is time, I glanced at the clock. You guessed it – 00:00. A time that has always held great significance to me personally, although I really couldn't say why.

I know it's illogical, but I have always hated that time – and would refrain from looking at the clock if I thought it was anywhere near midnight – just in case.

However, this time, it had caught me out, and it got me thinking...

The people – the ones that had occupied this space, *my space*, in years gone by – wouldn't even have known what 00:00 was!

Their time was analogue. Twelve of the clock, both hands pointing upwards. And then, what if my clock was wrong? – What if it were two minutes fast? Does that make my sighting of 00:00 irrelevant?

Well... *Yes*, it does!

And there's more.

What of so-called *Anniversary Hauntings*? The re-enactment of events long since passed. We've all heard of one, haven't we? That 'White Lady', whose forlorn ghost is said to appear every 4th of November, as she endlessly replays the scene of her untimely death.

Well, there's a problem.

Our yearly calendar has itself altered within recent history.

In 1752 our current Gregorian Calendar was introduced for the first time – changing the method used to calculate leap years, and thus creating a far more accurate calculation of the time it took for our Earth to orbit the Sun.

In order to compensate for centuries of previous inaccuracies, eleven full days were wiped from history in September of that year.

And that's surely got to change things?

That 'White Lady' from the 1600s... She returns every year on the anniversary of her sad demise... But does she show herself on the 4th of November, or should it now be the 15th?

So, I'm starting to get tangled in my thoughts.

If dates now are not the same as dates were then, and even the method by which we record time is, in itself, different – then surely, time should hold no significance for a haunting. And yet, still, anniversary hauntings are said to continue.

So, what *is* important?

What does it actually *need* for a replay haunting to take place?

I don't have the answer to that – but these days, I lean towards it having more to do with atmospherics, such as air pressure and the weather, lighting, and the mood of those present.

And for me... What now of 00:00?

With a little bit of logic and after a lifetime of superstition, it finally holds no significance for me at all.

## Chapter 5
# The Ghost Child & The 'Thing'

My Paranormal Experiences...

Your first real home – one that has your name on the mortgage papers at any rate, is a truly wonderful thing, and in my case, 'home', turned out to be a Victorian Semi, on the outskirts of the pretty Cornish village of St Agnes.

Our cheeky offer had been accepted, although, thinking back, it was ridiculously cheap – a real bargain. Had the lady selling it, maybe felt a little sorry for us? Whatever the reason though, I was grateful. It was in a bit of a mess to be honest. Lots to be done and no money to do it – but it was ours and we loved it.

We moved in with two young kids in tow. My daughter then would have been five years of age, and my son, just four. I don't know if you've ever tried it but restoring a property whilst entertaining young children is no easy feat and took pretty much all my time and energy.

The house was… how can I put it? ...*a little on the rough side*, I guess you'd say. It lacked plaster on some walls – had a very basic, rudimentary kitchen and no heating whatsoever. But life, for the most part, was good and we were happy there.

The first inkling that something *wasn't quite right*, apart from an odd pervading atmosphere that hung about the place at times, was the tapping.

I quickly realised, once I'd accepted its existence, that I'd actually been hearing it for quite some time – but it had been so feint, so subtle, that I just hadn't properly registered. I was tuned in now though, and it soon became apparent that it was always in a series of six. Six little taps. So soft – like fingernails on wallpaper and it didn't seem to matter where I was in the house – it could happen literally anywhere.

No big deal. Just tapping, right? – But then came the day that something snagged at the hem of my shirt. *Had it caught on something*? I looked about me, baffled. I was in the middle of the living room and there was simply nothing here for it to catch on.

More and more of those strange little *tugs* just kept happening, when it dawned on me – it finally clicked into place. I had to accept now that we were not alone here, and that we had probably *never* been alone. The house we thought we'd chosen, had maybe chosen us after all!

Days would go by, but then, there it was again... *tug tug... tug tug!*

I didn't speak up at first. I felt awkward about telling anyone – but the subject came up soon enough, when I noticed my husband flinch and fling his arm back behind him, as though shooing something away. He'd been sitting, cross-legged, in front of the television, playing the Sega Mega Drive. Yes... of course, we'd bought it for the kids, but the big kid had to try it out too, eh?

'You okay?' I was curious.

'No... Something keeps tugging at my shirt.'

So that was how it started, and it would happen at the strangest of times.

Like when my husband was sprawled on the floor. Play grappling with a four-year-old and shrieking with laughter as my daughter had piled in on top of the both of them. As I looked on, smiling at their antics, there it was again – *tug tug... tug tug*, and I quickly crossed the room, pressing my back firmly to the wall.

It was unnerving.

I was getting jumpy, and I wasn't the only one – so it was an easy joint decision to simply ask it to '*Stop.*'

I don't know why we thought it would work. In fact, I'm pretty damned sure that neither of us believed it *could* work – but work it did!

ALL clothes tugging and tapping simply stopped. Completely and totally – stopped.

We were overjoyed. This was great. We could get on with our lives and no longer feel uncomfortable in our own home.

Daily rough and tumbles went on unmolested – Mega Drive sessions could be concentrated on without fear of interruption, and I no longer felt the need to stand with my back to the wall, in the hope of deterring unwanted attention. *Fantastic*!

But humans are funny old things, and would you credit it – after weeks of non-events, we started to feel guilty.

That discussion, when it finally happened, was an odd one for sure.

'– But it's just a kid.'

'It's obvious that he only wants to play.'

Could we *really* tolerate it? – If it were to start up again?

Feeling nervous and not a little stupid, we sat down together in the living room and called out to the little boy. For no reason whatsoever, we both felt that it was, indeed, a boy.

'We're sorry we asked you to stop. It was just because you made us jump.'

'If you could try not to do that, you would be very welcome to join in with us again ...if you would like to.'

Well, we waited – and waited some more...

It took about three weeks, and then came the first,

tentative *tug tug*. He was communicating with us again! Yes, I know it sounds kinda weird, but we were actually delighted.

So go on… ADMIT IT!

…You're just dying to know about the '*Thing*' now, aren't you?

Life had returned to a strange sort of normality for our little family *(and by family, I am of course, including the extra one)*. It's extraordinary how quickly you can come to accept these things.

His presence wasn't something that either of us had ever discussed with other people though. No way was I going to open myself up to ridicule, by confessing to having a ghost boy in our house. Oh no – he would have to remain our little secret.

It was another event, months down the line however, that I need to tell you about now, and it's a strange one, for sure.

During the intervening months, we'd managed to pull at least some of the house into a semi-reasonable state, and at this point, we were the proud owners of a brand new, if minuscule, kitchen and the three bedrooms had all been finished to at least a basic level. The living room, though liveable, was far from complete, but the dining room was just a total mess.

There was no plaster on the walls and not too much on the ceiling either. The floor was rough concrete, and a liberal layer of builder's dust lay all around. Into this mess, we'd added a couple of boxes of, as yet, unpacked items, a dining table and a stack of chairs that were still waiting for somewhere to call home.

Best thing to do with this room?

Shut the door on it!

Except we couldn't. At least, not completely. The door had warped slightly over the years, and the catch wouldn't quite take, so leaving it ajar was the only real option.

So – I have set the scene for the arrival of my oldest, dearest friend.

My husband, doing that valiant thing that men do when their women get together to chat, went down the pub and left us to it!

It had been way too long since Sarah, and I had last seen each other, and we'd spent that evening catching up on our respective lives – laughing hysterically over old times and sharing long-forgotten memories.

All too soon, as is the way of things when you're having fun, evening turned into night, and it was time to head upstairs. Sarah was tired after her long journey, and we had a lot to do the following day.

So – flicking off the light switch, I followed her from the room.

And THAT was when we saw it... Well, to be honest – we *heard* it.

Sarah had her foot on the bottom stair, her hand still resting on the newel post, ready to climb. She'd stopped dead, and so had I.

A peculiar little *scrabbling, scratching* noise had grabbed our attention – and it was coming from the dining room.

'Did you hear that? – What is it?'

'I don't know.' I began creeping towards the dining room door.

I hadn't got far though, when we both clapped eyes on it – and shrieking, we about turned as one and took off up the stairs at a rate of knots.

There, towards the bottom of the door, had been a little brown '*arm*'. Shoved through the gap, it was questing – feeling around the door, as though trying to find a way through.

I honestly have absolutely no idea what the hell that thing was – but I can tell you what it wasn't. It was no mouse. It was no rat... or *anything* like that!

It had a human-like shape to the arm, with an elbow, wrist, and fingers, but it couldn't have been more than about six inches high!

There was no way in or out of that room, except via

the door – yet the following morning, when we felt *(with daylight and time passed)* able to deal with whatever it might be, we cautiously pushed open the door, only to find – nothing!

Now I have not mentioned this to many people in my life, and I really don't know what to make of it.

It has been suggested by some, that know far more of these things than I *(not really difficult, if I'm honest)*, that it could have been a House Brownie.

In common folklore, a Brownie is a small Hobgoblin or Fairy. They inhabit our homes yet go about their business unseen and undetected in our busy modern lives. Most are thought to be helpful, and will repair damaged items and tidy in the quiet of night – others though *(which would be more my luck, let's face it!)*, are mischief makers, bringing about chaos and havoc.

Now I don't believe in fairies – I mean, that's just silly, isn't it?

But then – I *do* believe my house to be haunted by the spirit of a little boy, who likes to play games with us!

It's just the word though... 'Fairy.' ...And Hobgoblin is obviously no better!

I'm sitting here, shaking my head and giggling to myself as I make myself write those words. Although I'm honestly not sure why I find them so much harder to accept than others – such as 'ghost', for example.

Come on – think about it logically, Allison!

I have already accepted that ghosts or spirits, can and do, show themselves in many forms – so why shouldn't this be just another form of manifestation?

Maybe, If I can get myself to think of it that way, I could come to accept their suggestion.

Oh, I don't know.

All I can say for sure, is that I have never seen the like of it before, nor since – and although twenty-four years have now gone by, neither me, nor Sarah have ever forgotten it.

Chapter 6

# So, You Think You'd Like To Be A Paranormal Investigator?

So, you're maybe thinking that you'd like to try this paranormal investigation malarkey for yourself?

Where do you go?

What do you do?

The first port of call should really be one of the many public events that you'll find advertised online or on social media.

No, it won't be the same as a proper, fully-fledged investigation – if only due to the high numbers of people that will inevitably be present – but it'll be near enough to give you an idea of whether or not it is actually right for you.

Keep your eyes open for local paranormal event organisers and ask for recommendations from friends and family. There can be huge variations on what is on offer, so choose a group that is prepared to talk you through safety, equipment uses, and – most important of all – they must be honest and never prone to theatrics or fakery.

So, what can you expect from the classic 'ghost hunt' or public paranormal investigation event?

Typically, after the meet and greet, there will be a short pre-investigation presentation on what the night may bring, and this is generally followed by a lit walk around.

This is an important part of the night. It will allow you to familiarise yourself with the site – to get to know the layout, the safety exits – and to draw your attention to any significant hazards. At this point, you'll also be given a brief history of the building and maybe, details of any strange events, previously reported in each area.

A group protection exercise of some kind should always follow – and is aimed at both protecting you from resident spirits, and at getting you in the zone.

This could take the form of standing in a circle. Holding hands and imagining a white light, flowing from person to person, directed around in a circular motion – with the aim being to strengthen the group's energy. Or maybe, they will ask you to internalise your thoughts – to imagine a particular scenario in your mind. This would be an attempt to get you into a more meditative state, which could enhance your chances of connecting with the spirit world.

Methods are many and varied, and each host will have their favourite.

After the team energy building exercises are complete and any final safety advice dispensed, there will be the opportunity to investigate in a small party, with an assigned team leader.

This is your time to investigate. Now it's *you* that will get to test out the equipment and attempt your own spirit communication. Do grab the opportunity to work with your host, though. Ask for their advice. They're there to help, so make the most of them.

Likely as not, they'll be able to show you a diverse range of communication techniques throughout the evening. See what piques your interest and don't be afraid to give it a go. And yes – I realise that some of those techniques can appear a little wild and wacky – but try them; you never know... Something they suggest, might just work perfectly for you. Everyone is different, after all.

Finally, towards the end of the night, there is often an opportunity to try out an individual investigation. Your chance to go it alone – in an area of your choice *(obviously, dependent upon the rules of the particular building that you are in)*.

So that, in a nutshell, is what you can expect on a

public ghost night – but to get the most out of the experience, here's a little advice...

As it is common to hold events in old historic places, they are inevitably unheated and often not even weatherproof. You will need to be well kitted out with sensible, comfortable shoes, many warm layers, and a torch is essential – as you'll be spending the majority of the night in the pitch black.

If you have any equipment yourself, then don't hesitate to take it along. It would be a great opportunity to try it out. But if nothing else – do bring your mobile.

You can use it to take photographs or to make notes. You'll have the torch function, of course, and if you load the right app, can even use it as a voice recorder – providing the opportunity of maybe catching an EVP *(Electronic Voice Phenomenon)* or two.

Just ensure that, on arrival, you remember to switch it to airplane-mode to prevent random phone signals from giving you any false positives.

Not all, but most paranormal events, will have at least one person with mediumistic capabilities present on the night. They can be valuable for settling people in and for giving an overview of what spirits may be around.

Don't be tempted though, to ask them to make contact with Great Aunt Gertrude. Obviously, this would be of significant interest for *you*, but a complete turn-off for everyone else present. And besides – wouldn't it be far more impressive, if she *(Aunt Gertrude)* were to be channelled by them completely unprompted?

One of the downsides of any investigation, be it public or private, is the presence of, what I refer to as a *Psychic Blocker*.

This is someone that is *completely* closed off to the paranormal world, either intentionally or otherwise – and their mere presence will mean that nothing is liable to happen.

Often, they themselves are *completely* unaware of the effect they can have on their surroundings – and it can be a real shame. They might genuinely want to have an experience – or they might be highly sceptical and scoff at the mere idea... Either way, it just isn't going to happen.

Talking of scoffing – one of the most important things that you can bring to an investigation *(apart from open-mindedness)* is respect. Respect for spirit, and respect for all others present.

If you absolutely, one hundred per cent, do not believe in even the *merest possibility* of the existence of ghosts... then stay away! Why waste your time and money? And worse still – why spoil the night for everyone else?

You'd think it a given, wouldn't you, that a total non-believer would stay away from a ghost hunt evening. But you'd be wrong. It happens all too often.

Anyway, rant over. Now, back to our investigation...

Apart from the use of various electronic gadgets and gizmos, there are a number of investigative techniques that you may come across or hear about during the night.

Usually referred to as the *Singapore Theory* – this is the use of specific items, sounds, words, or phrases that may have special meaning and relevance to spirit. It is an attempt to bring about increased activity, or direct paranormal communication.

Examples would be playing the music of the relevant period. Dressing in costume and maybe performing a re-enactment – or even blasting out the sound of an air raid siren. Whatever you choose, though, just try to make it relevant to wherever you are holding the investigation.

I have tried the air raid siren idea myself, on several occasions. Most recently, whilst at a nearby derelict WWII Control Tower.

On each occasion, I noted a significant change in atmosphere. It's like charging the air around you and is literally spine-tingling – and yes, it did bring on further activity for us. One of my meters was knocked clean off the shelf after one such experiment – narrowly missing me in the process.

A firm favourite with guests on a ghost hunt is the chance to try *Glass Divination*. Simply put, this is an attempt to communicate with spirit by using an upturned glass on a smooth glossy surface – such as a well-polished table.

Everyone taking part places one fingertip lightly on the base of the glass – with the idea being, to simply get the glass to move.

In order to build energy in the first place and get things going, participants will move the glass in large circles – whilst calling out for any spirit present to take over. Hopefully, you will soon begin to feel a *change* within the movements of the glass – and from that point on, should make no further attempt to influence its movements.

By asking spirit to choose a direction for 'yes', and another for 'no', a conversation, of sorts, can often be had.

Another all-time favourite with event guests, has to be *Table Tipping* – and it can be really dramatic at times.

As with the glass, participants position themselves around a small but sturdy table – placing their fingertips *(not hands)*, very lightly on the surface. Choose who is going to take the lead – then that person will attempt communication by asking spirit to move the table in response to their questions.

Yes, it sounds weird!

Yes – I guess *it is weird*. But it can also be quite spectacular at times.

If you are looking to try a more solitary method of

communication, however – then there can be few better than the use of either *Dowsing Rods* or *Pendulums*.

Both of these divining techniques can be accomplished without the help or influence of others – and at times, the results can be startling.

Dowsing rods are merely a length of metal (usually copper), bent into a right angle – with the smaller lengths being gripped loosely in an upright position, whilst the longer is left free to swivel.

With one held in each hand and the rods pointing forwards, communication can be achieved by asking spirit to move the rods, in direct response to questions asked. In order to get satisfactory answers though, it is first necessary to clarify 'what means what'.

Ask spirit to show you a 'yes.' If the rods cross, this will be the 'yes' answer – but they could stay straight – or even move further apart. Whatever they choose though, will be the 'yes' answer for the remainder of that session.

Now follow the same technique to assign the 'no' answer and once assigned, away you go with your questions.

Obviously, all questions will need to have a yes or no answer. Alternatively, you could ask for a direction – for example, 'where are you standing in the room?'

Using the pendulum is similar in technique.

Steady your arm *(I recommend resting your elbow on*

*something solid)*, dangle the pendulum from your fingertips and keep very still.

Communication can be achieved by the pendulum starting to swing clockwise, anti-clockwise, or by going back and forth. Again, you will need to predetermine which movement will mean 'yes' and which will be 'no'.

Before the night is over, don't forget to try some quiet time.

Take yourself off somewhere on your own *(if the size of the venue makes this a possibility, of course)* and just sit quietly and listen – to acclimatise yourself to the sounds of the building around you. Once ready, maybe you could start to call out, for a particular activity to occur. Ask spirit to tap on a wall, perhaps – or to show you a light anomaly. The possibilities are endless.

So, these are just a few examples of what you may come across on a typical public ghost hunt or paranormal investigation.

Try it out and see what works for you. See what fires your imagination.

Don't forget to take lots of photos throughout the night – and to look carefully at the results. You never know; you might just have caught something of interest – and if you have, don't be shy about sharing it with the event organisers.

They will always be keen to see potential evidence

and will happily offer advice and opinions on what you've caught.

You can, of course, share your findings on social media, if you've a mind to – but be aware that some may mock.

If that is likely to upset you, then maybe it is something best avoided.

Unfortunately, these days, it's become a normal part of life within the paranormal community – and there's just no getting away from it, I'm afraid.

Chapter 7
# The Bird And The Butterfly

My Paranormal Experiences...

It was in the fierce heat of a French high summer that I unexpectedly lost my mother – my beloved mum and best friend, all rolled into one.

For five years, she and my dad had lived alongside us in France, encouraging us in our endeavours and raising us up when we made mistakes along the way. They'd shared our dreams and had made our family complete.

She was a truly beautiful person, and kindness shone through her. A little bit of her remains still, residing within me, but never enough. I am, sadly, not the selfless, loving person that was my mother. No – the world lost a good soul that day.

It is difficult for me to write this, and to be honest, I would as soon rather not – but write it I must because it is relevant to my journey.

I don't need to go into details... I am sure you will have experienced the heart-wrenching effects of grief at some point in your life, but what I *do* want to talk about, was to happen a year after she had left us. One year to the day, to be precise.

It was early morning, and as was customary for me at the time, I was sitting at my desk in my home office – idly working through a few unanswered emails.

Seemingly out of nowhere, a tiny white butterfly appeared and began fluttering back and forth in front of me. Sweeping at it idly with one hand, I paid it no great heed – and yet it persisted – succeeding finally at grabbing my attention.

I watched, entranced, as it danced before me. It was beautiful and *so* tiny. I reached out a hand – but it easily evaded my touch, swooping downwards to settle on top of the small photo frame that had graced my desk – a frame that contained a favourite snapshot of my mum.

Crawling slowly downwards, it carefully centred itself right over her face – stopped, and then fully extended its wings. Finally at rest now and perfectly still.

I was spellbound, feeling an instant rush of warm energy surge through me. This was a message... it *had* to be a message. I looked up at the clock, somehow already knowing what I was going to see – 08:00. The very time of my mother's passing – one whole year before.

There was a sudden quiet in the world – and a

beautiful feeling of peace and love filled me as I regarded my tiny messenger.

A full minute or so must have passed as I gazed in wonder at its fragile beauty. Its tiny wings had been tinged with just a hint of shimmery blue and appeared almost translucent in their delicacy.

Then, abruptly, it took to the wing once more, danced around the room a couple more times and was away.

Message received, mum. Thank you so much.

That little winged emissary had brought me such a wonderful moment of peace and serenity, but it wasn't the only time that an animal messenger was to be used in this way. Two years later, in the June of 2009, I was to receive my next extraordinary visitation.

It was late in the day, coming dusk, and I was sprawled on the sofa in the living room, watching tv with my long-suffering husband. The two dogs were curled up on the rug – one, most likely Jack, was snoring softly – and the cat, Harry? Well, he was off doing whatever it is that cats do on a balmy summer evening.

A persistent light tapping worked its way into my consciousness, and my eye was drawn to the double glass doors of the hallway beyond. Something kept flitting in and out of view. 'What the hell...' I craned my neck to get a better look.

Curiosity piqued – I heaved myself off the chair and went to investigate.

It was a bird, a little chaffinch. And as I watched, it darted up and down – fluttered at the glass in front of me – before carrying on with its crazy aerial dance once more.

I laughed delightedly. Its antics were a joy to behold.

'What's it doing?' My husband appeared at my side, drawn by the sound of my laughter.

'I don't know. I guess there must be midges there or something.'

Well, it was unusual for sure, but no great mystery – so leaving it to its frolics, we returned once more to the telly and, soon enough, retired to bed for the night.

The next day dawned bright and clear. The sky was already a flawless bright blue, and a haze of heat shimmered in the distance. It was going to be an absolute scorcher – you just knew it from the start.

Alone in the house, I grabbed my marmite toastie and, taking a bite, made my way through to my office. Work to do...

My livelihood at that point in time, was an online silver jewellery business that my mum had helped me start up, and at that stage, just a few years in, it was finally starting to really take off.

Mid-bite, with one hand still on the door handle, I

stopped dead – letting the toast fall once more to the plate.

There, sitting on the flower-filled window box, was the chaffinch.

My beautiful little visitor fluttered up and away, startled by my sudden appearance, only to quickly compose himself and settle down once more – now gripping firmly to the crossbar of the window.

The cheeky little devil!

He stared straight at me, cocking his head in silent acknowledgement.

'Hello, my little friend. What are you up to?' Crossing to my chair, which was next to the window, I made to sit down.

In obvious fright, the alarmed bird darted across to the nearby damson tree – before hesitating – turning about, and promptly flying straight back.

He fluttered up and down, hovering against the glass of the window, before once more, taking up his position on the crossbar – peering at me with those dark, inquisitive eyes.

'Hey buddy, it's great to see you. You'd better keep an eye out for Harry, though... you'd make him a lovely breakfast.'

Delighted as I was by this unexpected caller, my concern was growing. If Harry – my *'Great White Hunter'*, otherwise affectionately known as *'Fat Cat'*, were to get him, it would just break my heart. Reaching across to open the window, I waved my arms wildly, intent on shooing him away.

The bird though, was having none of it. Clearly terrified, it kept darting off, only to return a few minutes later to his unwavering vigil at my window.

Okay then – have it your own way.

I tried taking no notice of him. I tried just getting on with my work, but if ignored too long, he would fly up to the crossbar again and give me that look – the one that seemed to say, 'oh no lady, you don't get to ignore *me*.'

So, the morning wore on, and my feathered friend and I passed it amicably enough – he outside the window, me within. Far too much of my work time was wasted that day though – as I became almost obsessed with capturing him on camera. And in truth, I did get some amazing shots. But then how could I not, when he was about a foot away from the lens – just the other side of the glass?

Lunchtime came and feeling peckish, I sauntered through to the kitchen. I had no more than opened a cupboard door though, when a familiar fluttering announced a presence at the glass of the kitchen door.

Oh, so you're following me now, are you?

Testing my theory, I continued through to the dining room. Yes – there he was, just a few short seconds and he'd found me again.

This was getting really weird now.

That whole day was spent in the company of my frightened little buddy. He was obviously doing something that terrified him, yet he'd stuck at it. Come late afternoon though, with a last knowing look and flutter at the glass, he was finally away.

I was both relieved and saddened to see him go. I had been so terrified about the cat – and that was weird in itself, thinking back... Where *was* Harry? He virtually always spent at least part of the day with me, usually draping himself inelegantly across the router on my desk.

So, what had driven the chaffinch, that gorgeous little fella, to undergo his epic surveillance session? I can only think it was my mum. In fact, I *knew* it was my mum. A medium had previously told me that she would attempt to make contact, but only when she believed me to be ready. I had to assume now, that she considered that I was.

The intense gaze from those shiny black eyes when that dear little bird had cocked his head and stared straight at me, had clearly seemed to say, 'Everything is alright. All is good.'

It was one of the more bizarre episodes of my life for sure, and one I could certainly never forget ...but then, sometimes life can be cruel and begin stripping away even our most precious of memories. If I *were* ever to start to doubt my recollections, though, in the years to come, I'll still have all those beautiful pictures to look back on, won't I? Just for confirmation, should I ever need it, that it did indeed occur.

Now I truly believe that those two events were communications from beyond, messages from my dear mum. Not just consisting of mere words but showing an extraordinary ingenuity in sending me the reassurance that I needed, a means of putting my mind at peace.

On those occasions, animals... (Hang on... is a butterfly an animal? Err – no. It's an insect! – Stupid woman!)

Okay – let's start again. On those occasions, an animal and an insect were somehow compelled to be used as messengers. But what happens when animals themselves have a message to send? – When *they* become the phenomenon?

In our pre-Harry *(Fat Cat)* years – and during the months immediately following the sad loss of our previous cat, Molly, both my husband and I would often catch sight of her still, out of the corner of our eye.

She would be following us around in the garden, trailing us wherever we went – just as she had done in life.

Sadly, she had ingested poison somewhere whilst out and about, and the vet had been unable to save her. She had died whilst on my lap, somehow still managing to raise her head and meow in answer to my own, until the end had mercifully come.

As a brightly coloured tortoiseshell, she had been unmistakable, and though it was but a glimpse, it was *many* such glimpses – and we were content with her continued presence.

It would be a good six to seven months before all further sightings finally stopped.

I guess that meant she'd finally moved on.


So, if our animal companions can be influenced into behaviours that are totally against their natures, and they can manage to stay with us, *even* after their passing – then do they maybe have a greater awareness of the spirit world than we do?

I believe the simple answer to that is *Yes!*

How many times have you glanced down at your cat, only to see it focussed intently on something. Behind you maybe, something that is simply not there.

Try waving your hand about to gain its attention or block its view, and it will crane its neck – continuing to look straight past you – intent only on maintaining eye contact with whatever has drawn its gaze.

I had an intriguing experience with the dogs once, at

a holiday cottage we'd rented a good few years back. Well... at least, my father did.

We'd all gone to the pub for the evening – leaving him happily watching tv in the company of the two dogs. An uneventful hour had passed, when suddenly, they'd both leapt up from where they'd been curled up asleep on the rug and had literally flung themselves at an apparently empty space next to the window, barking, snarling, and growling menacingly in warning.

It had undoubtedly put the wind up my dad, who had already been uneasy in the weird atmosphere of the place. He'd been so glad to see us back.

Safety in numbers and all that!

Another occasion involving my dog, however, was to happen entirely the other way around.

I was alone in my home of the time (a tiny Cornish cottage some three hundred years old) and had been sat on the floor in the living room, engrossed in going through a box of LPs. *(Yes – I am that old!)* My dog, snoozing contentedly by my side.

Oblivious to all but my search, I was still thumbing my way through when suddenly there was a tremendous crash from above – and I mean LOUD! I literally felt the vibrations through the floor as I sprang to my feet *(oh, how I miss being able to do that)*, my heart beating wildly in my chest *(that bit, I could do without though – truth be told)*.

*What the hell was that?*

It had sounded like the wardrobe had fallen over or something...

Gathering my nerve – I crept up the old stairs, and before I could convince myself otherwise, quickly stuck my head into the back bedroom – a room I always avoided if I could, as it just felt *wrong*. But the wardrobe was still standing, and everything was in its place.

Feeling more confident now, I quickly checked out my bedroom – but again, everything was as it should be. What could have made that crash?

Perplexed, I trudged back down the stairs and returned to the living room, flopping inelegantly onto the sofa.

I looked again up at the ceiling, puffing out my cheeks. What could have even made that much noise? It had literally vibrated through the floor! I shook my head in confusion, as the dog still snoozed contentedly.

Then it hit me – the dog! The dog hadn't reacted to the crash!

Not at all.

He hadn't so much as twitched an ear.

Now I truly believe animals to be on a higher spiritual level than us mere humans. But sometimes – just occasionally, it can be the other way around.

Chapter 8

# The Pitfalls - Tales Of The Unexpected

(The Hazards of Being a Paranormal Investigator)

Oh, the life of a paranormal investigator...

Is it glamorous? – No!

Is it exciting? – Usually not.

Then why do we do it?

I think most of us would agree that it becomes a compulsion. Once you have the paranormal bug, it's there for life – and the very thought of missing an investigation! Ugh! It's enough to make your blood run cold. But for those yet to experience the thrill of the chase – here's a few hazards that you *might* not have considered yet.

**Spiders And Bugs**

Oh, the joy... The absolute delight of spending our

precious free time in dark and derelict buildings – with their fresh outdoor facilities and wall-to-wall bug runs.

But it's those lucky few investigators... those few courageous martyrs of the curse that is arachnophobia – *the likes of me!* – that will get to experience the true spine-tingling terror of a paranormal night-time investigation.

Yes, at times, things can get *really* interesting out there.

That blood-curdling scream that you picked up on the recorder is not in fact, a ghostly re-enactment of past atrocities – but just me – when I accidentally point the night vision camera downwards and spot an eight-legged nasty crawling up my fleece.

*Now I know what you're going to say* – 'Don't be such a big baby, Allison. They're really friendly; just look at that sweet little face...'

Yeah, yeah, yeah...

Well, let me tell you – there is *nothing* sweet about those horrible hairy horrors. They're monstrous – and I couldn't look one in the eye if I tried. I mean... which eye would I even look at? *They've got eight of them!* – And besides, what if it were to take direct eye contact as a challenge? The absolute last thing I'd want, would be to risk provoking an attack.

Shadow figures and disembodied whispers are fine – but spiders...? No Way!

## The Cold

Until you've done a few overnight investigations in the depths of winter, you have no idea just how bitterly cold it can get out there.

We're often in windowless damp places, with nowhere dry to sit and few places to get out of the wind. Blue extremities are the sign of a hardened investigator – and learning to set up the camcorder with hands that won't stop shaking is all part of the joy. When that cold has seeped into your very bones, even an electric blanket on your return home, can't touch it.

And with that cold, of course, comes the wind.

It can ruin recordings and create havoc with filming – and I'm not just talking about appearing on camera with your hair sticking up like you've been plugged into 240v *(although that, too, is obviously a trauma)*.

## Night Vision Cameras

Never forget that these things can see where we cannot. They sit there, patiently waiting for you to do something stupid, and then capture it on film for the immense enjoyment of others.

Those of you who know me personally (*very personally in this case*), will know that I had a particularly spectacular run-in with a night vision camera placed in the Ladies' toilet of a well-known haunted pub.

Guess who forgot it was there?

Yep - it had to be me!

**The Public**

Often, the places we go have full public access – and although we obviously usually go under cover of darkness, so do some other, more nefarious members of society.

I live in constant fear of being stopped by the police and asked to explain why I have a night vision camera in a known 'dogging' spot.

'...But honestly, officer, I am just trying to film ghosts!'

**Egos**

What can I say about this? I don't think there can be anything more extraordinary on this Earth, than the ego of some paranormal investigators. They investigate ghosts... therefore – we must bow down before them, for they are God!

I have always done my best to stay away from narcissistic people. However, even I have been taken in on occasion ...for a while at least.

Don't let anyone tell you they are an expert, for there

is undoubtedly no such thing. Yes, plenty of people are very experienced and know a lot about the field, but they would also be among the first to agree that they are *'no expert'*.

A LOT of people talk the talk... Be careful who you listen to.

**Ghost Apps**

Ah, the bane of every investigator's life!

**No**, an app *can't* tell you if a ghost is approaching, and how malevolent it might be. Neither can it speak to the dead or send you a message from Great Aunt Augusta.

It can, however, create a neat little, totally fake photo of a ghost, zombie or the like, and cause genuine paranormal photos to be dismissed as *'just another fake'*, amongst the plethora of rubbish.

**Trolls**

Charming people... Not!

If you insist on getting involved in the paranormal scene, you will be hard put to avoid these *'wonderful'* people altogether. Just why they think they have a God-given right to make other people's lives miserable – heaven only knows. I surely don't.

Just be prepared to keep your distance from social media, or you'll need to grow a very thick skin.

## The 'Nutter' Value

I don't think it will really come as a shock to you, if I say that telling people what you do, will typically involve an awful lot of eye-rolling and accompanying sniggering. It just goes with the territory, I'm afraid. Best bet is to just avoid the subject altogether – with certain people, anyway.

On the flip side – of course, just as many people will love what you do and be drawn to you because of it. Although I'm not really sure if that's a good thing either. – I guess only time will tell.

## Parking

What? Wait... *Parking?*

Yeah, yeah, PARKING! I haven't completely lost the plot.

Well – maybe just a little, eh?

When out on an investigation, please take care where you decide to leave your car. Choosing the wrong spot could land you in a whole lot of strife.

At a recent investigation, we'd left ours on a deserted country lane, and had set out to walk the mile or so to our very rural location for the night – an abandoned and now derelict railway station, and nearby tunnel. On our return though, we were concerned to see blue lights flashing in the distance – and hurrying along, it soon became obvious that they were within the vicinity of the car.

Had there been an accident? Could someone maybe have driven into it?

Worried now, we upped the pace and came crashing out of the undergrowth and piled onto the lane – nearly giving the attending officer a heart attack as we did so.

As it turned out, we had unknowingly managed to park the car close to the home of the commanding officer of a nearby military base – and the police had been sent to check if we were a threat.

Well... We quickly explained who we were and where we had been, much to their very evident amusement.

'Hey – you should go try that. You're into that stuff,' one officer remarked to the other.

'I'm not scared of ghosts,' came the reply. 'Just of nutters, roaming around the countryside and popping out of hedges in the dark!'

Well, that's us!

We are those nutters – and long may it continue.

## Chapter 9
# Psychics & Mediums

The Opening up of a Whole New World...

My natural inclination here is to slip into the conversation that I'm actually not a medium – but undeniably more of a large *(unfortunately)* – But that would just be silly, so I won't do it!

Truth be told, I have never quite known what to make of mediums. I swing wildly between incredulity and awe, depending on which particular one I'm talking about.

But what exactly *is* a medium? I hear you cry.

Essentially here, I need to talk about two differing abilities – that of the psychic and that of the medium. The two differ quite dramatically yet remain forever intertwined and often coinciding.

All mediums are psychics, *of a sort at least* – yet not all psychics are capable of being mediums.

A psychic relies upon 'reading' your human aura, your mind or spirit – *your very essence*, if you will. Simply put, they read YOU!

They achieve this by tapping into a spiritual plane. Sometimes with the help of trigger objects like tarot cards, crystal balls or tea leaves – but more commonly, just by using a sort of extrasensory sixth sense – and when successful, are able to *see* and pass on information about your past, present and future.

Psychics will use many techniques to get a reading – sound, smell and even taste would you believe? – But when making a connection through *touch*, it is known as psychometry.

Psychometry is the extraordinary ability to acquire information simply by touching an item. The psychic might receive impressions of past emotions or pick up on who the item had belonged to. On occasion, they could even gain full awareness of past events – events that had happened whilst the object had been present.

It's based upon the theory that we leave a psychic imprint on the things that we come into contact with. On items that mean something to us – or were maybe present in our lives during a particularly traumatic or emotional time – be it good, or bad.

During a reading, psychics will assist you to ask spirit

simple questions – such as, 'Will I marry?' 'Will my career take off?' Or maybe even – '*Will I ever finish writing this book?*'

They can also attempt to *read* your future and to offer guidance on upcoming events. You must bear in mind, though, that the future is constantly changing, evolving – as we choose whether to accept or reject a particular path. Ultimately, we all have free will to determine our paths.

A medium, on the other hand, can use and tap into the same psychic world *(although not all will perform psychic readings),* but can now take that ability one stage further, and directly communicate with the spirit world itself.

You will still be able to ask your questions – but this time the answer is not being drawn from *your* psyche – but instead, comes directly from the spirits connected to you or from those around you – *in your space*.

The medium may simply divulge information about past events – affecting either you, someone you care about – or maybe concerning your home or immediate surroundings. It is a possibility, though, that they could pick up on the presence of passed family members – and if so, may even be able to pass on messages or offer words of comfort and guidance directly from them.

Mediums have the ability to channel spirit – to allow spirit to talk through them – to use their voice or body.

This can be done by entering into a trance *(think, old black and white photos of mediums, exuding ectoplasm from every orifice, here)*. These days though, that is unusual, and most now stay fully conscious and in the present whilst communicating.

As you can clearly see, the worlds of the psychic and that of the medium are forever intertwined – for the sake of ease however, I shall just use the term medium from this point on.

So, has your interest has been piqued?

Would you like to get a reading for yourself? – Or maybe you're hoping to make contact with someone dear to you?

If so, here are a few guidelines – a little help in finding the right person.

First and foremost – do your research. Find out how long they've been practising, check for recommendations and follow them up.

Look at their claims. If they maintain that they have a one hundred percent success rate with prediction accuracy – can always make contact with loved ones – or even that they could inspire that special person *(you know... that one you've your eye on forever)* to fall in love with you – then walk away. In fact, don't walk – run!

No one is able to make contact all the time. It just doesn't happen that way ...and of course, no one can ever be made to love you. Just as you have free will to create your own future – so do they.

So – research done, recommendations taken on board and not a dubious review to be seen. You've found the one – the person you've been looking for.

Before the session – think long and hard about your question and set guidelines on just how much information you are prepared to offer upfront.

On the day, give them your question or explain what it is that you need to know – but then try to remain silent, and as expressionless as possible – to avoid giving away your feelings about any direction in which they are taking.

Don't allow them to ask you too many questions or let them lead you into giving away more information than you had originally intended – they *really* shouldn't need it anyway.

Remain sceptical, and don't accept generic responses, such as, 'your mother loved you very much.' – *Of course,* your mother loved you! Instead, try to dig down – to get that bit of information that nobody else could possibly have known.

In my too numerous years in this mortal realm, I have had many mediums attempt to tell me what my future holds – where I'm going to live and what I'm going to be doing – but none have *really* grabbed my attention.

None that is, until I decided on the spur of the

moment to put my faith in Chris Conway – who I'd become aware of through watching early episodes of Most Haunted. *(Okay, okay... I'm over it now!)*

As I recall... he'd posted an offer of readings for just £5 – which was quite frankly, ridiculously cheap, considering the time and effort that he was going to need to put into it – and truthfully, I just couldn't resist.

All that was needed on my part, was to give him my question – one question – and at that time, there was really only one thing on my mind.

My French Farmhouse had already been on the market for four years, and although I'd had loads of interest, the right buyer still hadn't come along. I desperately wanted to return home, so my question was simple – 'When will I move back to Cornwall?'

With little expectation, I sent everything required – and pushing it to the back of my mind, just got on with daily life.

A few days later – hearing that little ping that indicated I'd received a new email – I glanced up from my paperwork and seeing Chris's name in the message preview, gave a wry smile. It was daft, I know, but hell, it was only a fiver!

I opened the message and began to read:

'The sale of your property has already begun in the mind of your purchaser. They have seen it, want it, and will make contact soon. The property sale will be confirmed within the month of September, and you will have returned to Cornwall by the end of the year.'

Wow – I chuckled to myself. *This is great!*

I told my husband and then promptly forgot about it. It was a lovely *idea* but highly unlikely in the real world, eh?

Oh, ye of little faith. Just how wrong could I be?

In the end – it was just three weeks later that I received the notification – that I got that email.

'We have been seriously looking at the details of your lovely home and have completely fallen in love with it. If still available, we would like to offer you the full asking price. We are unable to visit at this time, as we live in Dubai and have no leave due – but we are fully committed to the purchase and are willing to commence the sale through our solicitor and to forward any deposits necessary.'

*Oh my God*, it was really going to happen!

I looked again at the reading that Chris had given me. We were now the end of August – they had already decided to buy it in their minds. The timescale just fit.

It's fair to say, that we were utterly overwhelmed by that email. It had changed our whole life, and I enthusiastically began searching for our new home in our much-desired Cornish moorland village.

Well – the provisional contract *was* signed in September. The sale went through early December – and we finally moved back to Cornwall on the twentieth, just in time for Christmas.

I will always remain awestruck by the incredible accuracy of this amazing reading – and I really couldn't recommend Chris highly enough.

I think it safe to say that I now have a much greater respect for the capabilities of mediums. How could I not?

Two particular mediumistic talents that I greatly admire but remain forever outside my capabilities – are that of clairaudience (the ability to hear spirit), and clairvoyance (being able to see spirit).

I have met a good few people over the years that seem to possess these talents by the bucket load. Sometimes – sadly, they even seem unaware of the exceptional nature of their abilities.

Many is the time that I have expressed my desire to possess this talent – this ability – only to be firmly put back in my place.

'You don't want it – just be happy as you are.'

Or, the inevitable, 'You really don't want to see the things that I have.'

But they're wrong. I *do* want to see!

Nothing is more frustrating to me, than being able to *feel* a presence – to *know* something is nearby – yet to have no idea who, or what it may be. And worse still, I simply detest the thought that somebody else may know more about me than I do myself!

But, hey-ho, such is my lot in life, eh?

To be fair though, I obviously do have at least a small amount of *limited* psychic ability – as of course, does my daughter.

As I have just this moment stated… I *do* feel the presence of spirit – I *have* heard the odd set of disembodied footsteps – and I *have* had more than my fair share of paranormal experiences.

*So, shut up, Allison!*

I really do have little to complain about in the grand scheme of things.

One thing that always delights me, is unexpectedly coming across somebody gifted when I'm out and about – just going about my day-to-day life. To have someone, out of the blue, say, 'You know you have someone with you now, don't you?' And then to go on to describe who it is, that they see… It's simply incredible.

Like that gypsy woman – being able to tell my mother about the 'haunted' writing desk. It's just so *random* that it's mind-blowing.

And being informed by a local medium that a traumatic event was the cause of activity in our French gîte. *(I bet you were still wondering about that one… weren't you?)*

Well, the tale turned out to be an odd one – and so very sad.

She'd told me, that she could hear shots – that sounded like musket fire – coming from the woods beyond, but it was getting louder ...closer.

That there was a young girl, running wildly – and she kept looking back behind her, towards the woods. She was desperate to get away, to escape from the soldiers – but she wasn't quick enough. She had been caught, beaten and quite brutally raped – resulting in an unwanted pregnancy.

In the following months, the girl had kept to herself – hiding her growing belly as best she could, whilst she slowly recovered. When the pains came – she had let herself into our barn and there, alone had given birth to her premature and stillborn child.

Wrapping that child tenderly in a blanket, she had placed the baby in the far corner of the unused building, and covering it reverentially with straw, had turned and walked away.

The activity, she'd told me *(how did she even know about that?),* was because of the guilt the girl had felt about abandoning her baby in this way.

She returns, to care for the child.

Well... that'd do it, eh?

I need to add here, that the medium in this case,

knew nothing of the hauntings – of the reports from our guests or indeed, that we had any activity *at all*.

I had merely asked her if she could pick anything up, as we had strolled around the property.

So – that 'back part of the barn' is now the oft-shunned back bedroom.

Could this, perhaps, explain why activity would ramp up whenever the door to that room was kept closed? It's certainly feasible. Maybe, she didn't like the idea of her child being shut away again?

To balance things out a bit though – I do have to add that most 'on the spur' readings that I have been offered, were usually way off the mark.

I have been told that my father will remarry (*never gonna happen*). That we will live in a large house with many acres of land (*in my dreams!*). That I will become successful and fulfilled *(please ask ALL your family and friends to buy a copy of this, and who knows?)* and finally that my mum says, 'We should eat more bananas!'

YES - I'm serious!

Well – they were bang on with that one, at least.

See? That little bit of information that nobody else could possibly have known.

Chapter 10
# It's All About The Energy
Some More of my Musings...

Over the years, I have come to the conclusion *(not proven fact, of course, but simply my own personal thoughts)* that life, death and pretty much everything in between, is all about energy

Not the sort that comes in copper cables and enables our comfortable modern lifestyle – but the kind that flows in, around and through *everything*.

Think Avatar here (only without the need to plug your hair into a bleddy great tree – I mean... obviously!), I actually believe they may have, somehow, tapped into my mind.

Energy drives literally everything, from a molecular level, to complex lifeforms. It heats our world and floods the Earth with life-sustaining oceans, creating, in its path, the necessary plant life needed for the animal world to thrive.

That very energy, the energy that we need to *exist* – runs throughout us. It powers our movements, regulates our temperature, and fires the synapses in our brain – allowing complex thought and enabling movement. Without it, we mere humans are nothing but meat-covered bones.

When we die, that energy leaves our body – that's a given. But here's the thing...

The First Law of Thermodynamics states that energy can change from one form into another but can neither be created nor destroyed. *And* that the amount of energy and matter contained within the Universe remains a constant – just endlessly shifting from one form to another.

So, if the body has died, where does all that energy go?

All those thoughts, personality traits and memories? They couldn't have existed without energy – they have been created by energy – they *are* energy and if that energy can't be destroyed, then it must still exist – just in another form.

Could it be possible that it's this transformation of energy that we've come to think of as The Paranormal? ...When the energy *(soul if you like)* of a once living person gets redirected back into the ether? That's certainly the direction that my thoughts take me.

For me, it's not unusual to experience a 'buzz' of energy – that strange crawling sensation that's not unlike a powerful static charge – and it can literally make my hair feel as though standing on end. Well – arm hair, anyway *(Let's not be too over dramatic, eh?)*.

It can happen during an investigation, whilst visiting one of those beautiful old historic houses that I'm so fond of – or occasionally, even whilst walking down the high street on a seemingly otherwise uneventful day. Could these occurrences, these brief spikes of energy, somehow denote a place of power – if only in that one brief instant?

This spike, or surge, is a feeling I've come to know well. One that, for me, signals the presence of something spiritual – not necessarily paranormal per se – but definitely something out of the realm of the ordinary.

But what could *cause* these energy spikes?

I mean, yes – it could be that I have just encountered a spirit, or maybe it's some sort of residue of past energy build-up – a leftover, if you like, of some highly charged event – something traumatic maybe? Whatever it is though, it's strong. Strong enough to leave an imprint. A psychic footprint.

So, if you accept that the very *essence* of a once living person has now reverted back to energy, what would it then need, in order to interact with *us*, on our earthly plane?

More energy? Well... *Yes!*

We already know that spirit can and will, draw on any available power source in order to manifest.

On investigations, this could take the form of sapping the vigour and strength of any or all present – often leaving us feeling weak and sickly. More commonly, and I have no idea how, they will literally drain all available batteries and power packs – and the speed at which they can do it, is astonishing.

So, are they using us and our equipment as some kind of battery? Have we, ourselves, just become a paranormal power pack?

Let's suppose for a moment, that they *are* using us, as a power source. Are they doing it to make themselves stronger? Maybe in an effort to enable easier communication – or is it simply a way of *forcing* an awareness of their presence upon us?

In all honesty, it's probably a bit of both.

Who knows – maybe I'm way off the mark.

Maybe communication is the last thing they're concerned with – and they are just using our energy, our life force, as some sort of vampiric feast – whilst we, ourselves, are irrelevant to the act. In fact – I'm pretty sure that happens too on occasion.

At times, it's actually possible to measure these

spikes of energy that can literally stop us in our tracks. One bit of kit that is commonplace in the paranormal field and can do just that, is an EMF meter. The Trifield, or better yet, the Mel Rem, are both good examples – and both are superb devices for providing a visual sign that what you are feeling is real.

Sometimes however, technological gadgetry is simply superfluous to requirements. One such instance that comes to mind, was when my teammate and I were merrily chatting away, as we headed towards the arched granite doorway of a derelict and roofless church, in rural South Devon.

We reached the entrance still engrossed in conversation, but the moment we crossed that threshold, we both stopped dead – literally, mouths dropping open – as we looked at each other in stunned surprise.

That energy, the power that we had just walked into, was simply phenomenal – and it didn't need words or a fancy meter to tell us that we had *both* felt it.


There are places on this crazily spinning planet that we are fortunate enough to call home, where energy is naturally concentrated. Where pathways of invisible force, commonly known as Ley Lines, criss-cross the globe – creating a kind of network – a grid.

The points where these paths converge are believed

to be places of power and, historically, were often marked by the addition of shrines or places of worship – be it a grand gothic cathedral or a simple hermitage. Most of the world's more important historical monuments and monoliths can effectively be linked back to it.

Of particular significance to me, though, is the sheer abundance of paranormal phenomena documented at these sites. Could it be, that these places, too, are some sort of *paranormal filling station* – an earthly power point, if you like?

Energy can show itself in many forms – and light is one such state – so what of light anomalies? Those annoying little things known as orbs!

What many people deem to be an orb is, in fact, far more likely to be merely a particle of dust – reflecting on the light from the camera or some other source of nearby illumination.

There has become a kind of mania about this subject, however – with many investigators coming down firmly on the side of there being no such thing! But I am not one of those people.

Yes – I am aware that ninety-nine percent will be dust or filament particles, suspended in the air current – and yet there are some, at least, that cannot be explained away so easily.

One notable example was seeing two side-by-side

EMF meters simultaneously light up and alarm, in response to an orb swooping between them.

The anomaly, the 'orb', was only picked up in night vision, during an evidence review session – and had not been seen with the naked eye at the time.

Now – if this orb had affected both meters, as clearly seemed to be the case, then it must surely have been a source of energy – and no simple speck of dust.

Another orb sighting occasion that I find myself unable to debunk, is when two seasoned investigators were seated comfortably *(if such a concept exists)* within the cellars of Bodmin Jail. We were pre-investigation, and the lights were still on. Just sitting there chatting – casually watching as a faint green orb slowly meandered its way up the stone wall directly in front of us.

It was around maybe two centimetres across and was performing a slow, seemingly deliberate crawl up that wall – disappearing only when it neared the top. As I recall, it probably took about a minute to complete its journey.

Sometimes, and this is an odd one for me, I have encountered light that has no apparent light *source*. One such occasion was whilst travelling home from an investigation.

Sitting in the back seat, I was quietly peering out the window, into the darkness of the Devon countryside – when something caught my eye. Ahead of us was a strange pale blueish glow, and as we came closer, I came to realise where it was emanating from.

Just before you get to the Cornish border – there is a well-known steep-sided hill, crowned by a circle of trees. A somehow magical place – and known by all who live in Cornwall as The Nearly Home Trees.

I shouldn't have been able to see them in the dark and yet, clearly, I could.

The crowns of these trees were softly lit from within, and the bare winter branches were glowing a faint consistent pale blue. And yet, there was no source – no point of origin for the light.

I can't explain this – yet I've seen the phenomenon before – in a tiny ancient farmstead on the edge of the moor, decades earlier.

I had rented a gorgeous little granite farmhouse for a week. Standing, secluded, in the middle of a large open meadow and bordered on three sides by wooded hills with the river Camel running along the fourth. It was a feast to behold and such a beautiful, peaceful place.

Completely isolated from any external light source, the nights there were black indeed. Yet this night, as I lay in my bed, I suddenly became aware that I could see the A-beams.

Normally Indiscernible within the black of the room, they were now plainly lit – and obviously from outside the window as I could clearly make out the darker shadows of the beams, themselves, thrown onto the ceiling beyond.

Was someone in our meadow? It was the middle of the night, for God's sake!

Climbing wearily out of bed, I crossed to the window and put my hand to the pane, to block any glare. But there was no glare. All was black. Not even a hint of a light source – nothing.

Now I don't profess to know what these occurrences mean – or what they could be caused by. I don't know. Maybe it was some kind of spirit light – a memory perhaps, of a past time – when someone may have stood outside with a lantern and had softly lit the room within.

I include them here only because they are light energies – of unknown and, therefore, paranormal origin.

So, let's move on – to another energy – to sound.

Sound is just energy in the form of sound waves or vibrations – which can and will affect all it comes into contact with.

If spirits *(ghosts, if you like)* are energy – and sound is energy – then it stands to reason that spirits are able to create noise. All those bangs and raps that we hear on investigations...

Like when four of us were sat in a little circle in that same dank cellar in Bodmin Jail. Suddenly a loud, unnerving dragging sound came from our right. Our heads shot around as one – ears straining in the darkness.

As soon as it ended, an eerily similar sound erupted from our left – again, our heads shot round – eyes huge. The sound petered out – but only to come a third time, from straight ahead of us on this occasion.

Something was having fun with us for sure! We already knew there was nothing loose down there that could have been used to make those noises. No chests, tables, or chairs.

So, this was sound energy – seemingly coming from nowhere and produced with great effectiveness – but in order to do what?

Make us scared?

To let us know they were there?

As ever – who knows…


So those bangs and raps – those phantom lights – the footsteps and even that disembodied voice… they are all in their way, one and the same.

Light is an energy.

Sound is energy.

Thought is an energy.

And we… well, are you getting with the theme yet?

Chapter 11

# Home Again ...In Cornwall

My Paranormal Experiences...

Here I am, back in my beloved Cornwall at last – after ten long incredible years of living in the sun. Do I regret those years away from home? Not at all. They had given me a whole new experience of life, one that I would never have dreamed possible. A life full of laughter and wacky ex-pat parties and, of course, more than a little strife too, over that same time.

The one thing I *do* regret, however, is having to leave my daughter behind. But she is an adult now, and her life is her own to choose. I just wish she'd chosen Cornwall.

I love this place.

This quaint little moorland had always held a unique fascination for me – a special place in my heart. Tiny by the standards of the great Yorkshire Moors or by Dartmoor in neighbouring Devon, but this was where my heart lay ...where the low-lying marshes would rise up into those distinctive craggy, granite-topped tors and the gorse gives way to windblown heathers.

I took to exploring with great enthusiasm. Loving the freedom that having access to all that unspoilt beauty brought me and in particular, that I could begin my adventures right from my door, without need of a car.

Roughtor, Garrow Tor, Hawk's Tor, I loved them all – and there was no finer way to pass the day than sitting on those boulder-strewn heights, just watching the heavy clouds scudding by.

Then, there were the special places – those hidden places that seemed somehow to ooze an ancient power. It might be an innocuous-looking area of sparse woodland – yet it held an energy within – hidden and secretive somehow. It could be on the summit of a small insignificant tor – or maybe even in one of the many ancient stone circles that littered the landscape.

There are just so many circles to find out there, and I have been to most of them now. They somehow call to me, seeming to draw me into their embrace.

One fine morning I awoke, full of energy and determination, and had set off at daybreak to locate a particular circle – that I knew to be on the lower slopes of the ancient neolithic settlement at Leskernick Hill.

I knew where it was *meant* to be, I had spotted it on

the ordnance survey map just the day before, but now I was here, I couldn't see *anything*.

Up down, left, and right, I slogged – hiking back and forth, trying to spot my elusive target.

Where the hell was it?

Stopping to draw breath, I let my shoulders sag and my arms fall heavily to my side. Despondent now and just about ready to give up on my search, I glanced behind me, to the hilltop – shocked to see that a thick impenetrable mist was fast rolling in. I could barely see the boulders, and as I looked on, the valley below was already starting to disappear beneath me.

It would be stupid to risk staying out in that. Sighing dejectedly, I turned towards home and trudged off down the hill.

I hadn't got far though, maybe fifty, sixty yards, when a jolt of energy shot right through me – as I clearly felt that *buzz*. I shuddered as goosebumps ran down my arms – and even my scalp felt tingly.

But why? There was nothing here.

Looking around, I noticed the stump of a stone, all but hidden in the long, late summer grass. Then I saw another – and another!

As I spun around, I realised that I had stumbled, quite by chance, right into the centre of the very circle that I had been searching for.

The degraded and robbed-out stones were now little

more than stumps, and far too many were missing altogether – but oh, the power it held in that moment.

I stood still, arms outstretched – breathing in a beautiful peace. It's a good job that the mist *had* come – and that no one could've seen me, eh?

To be fair though, I have always had my little rituals in these most sacred of places. It's like, I have to touch each of the stones, in turn – to *feel* their energy.

And I'm certainly not the only one to feel this way about these places. I have met many with similar passions over the years.

Some stone circles on the moor are still actively used – for what exact purpose? I know not – although it does appear, to my eyes, to be vaguely 'witchy' in nature.

I have, when approaching one of the larger circles, seen someone hasten to leave – scurrying off and disappearing over the ridge of the hill before I could get too close. *Had that been a cloak they'd been wearing?*

Whatever... they obviously hadn't wanted my company. I continued on my way, ambling into the stones.

In the middle of the circle, lying on the centre stone, I found the offerings... Carefully arranged stones with strange symbols painted on them – broken bits of pottery and several flower heads. Hmmm.

You just never know what you're going to come across, do you?

You have to keep your wits about you when you're out

there, though – that's true enough. That moorland mist can come in an instant – fuelled, I guess, by the humidity in the air, meeting the wet marshy ground or something like that.

Anyway, without sight of the distant tors by which to navigate, it can get really disorientating. Even knowing the walks as well as I do, I have still managed to do a complete 180, to find myself walking in completely the wrong direction.

Over time, I have found it easier not to talk about my moorland explorations with my friends. If I share too much, they get concerned and start worrying about me being out there alone – afraid of what might happen. I mean... yes, there *are* many physical dangers – to me, though, it's just home.

That said, there *are* parts of the moor that feel different. Strange – somehow *dark*. These are the places that I avoid on foot – and when driving through remain the only places where I have ever locked the car doors.

I'm really not sure why, though. It's not as if a locked door would help me against anything paranormal, obviously! But I guess it, just eases my mind.

You'd be forgiven for thinking this feeling of unease is just in my head. But no – others have remarked upon it too. They can feel the wrongness. I have no idea of its cause, but it's definitely there. It would be fascinating, though, to visit these spots alongside someone with mediumistic abilities one day, eh?

My great love of the moor, and that sense of belonging, is unquestionably shared by my daughter. Like me, she too could lose herself for hours, simply sitting on a boulder, staring out across the open moorland to the tors beyond.

Now a mother of her own, she and my son-in-law had arrived with my two gorgeous granddaughters, for a much-anticipated family visit.

Our home now was a 1980's chalet bungalow, nothing special to look at from the outside, it's true – borderline ugly, in fact – but oh, such glorious views! It was like the world was spread out before you. It was the main reason we had chosen it. Well... that and its proximity to the moor, of course.

Inside, we'd been working hard on making it our own – tearing out walls and reconfiguring the awkward layout. We'd put in a newly fitted kitchen and remodelled the bathrooms, creating a bright, cheery and comfortable home.

And although virtually a new build, when compared with our French house, this new place of ours, was to turn out to have its own little secrets, after all.

Every night, when she got up to do the night feed for

the baby, my daughter would become aware of the sound of quiet talking – of whispering.

Perplexed, she'd eventually asked us why we were always talking in the middle of the night? Had we been disturbed by the baby?

'No... it's not us,' we'd assured her.

Luckily *(for us)*, we had been blissfully sleeping throughout. Unaware, for the most part, of her nightly vigils.

That next night, feeling edgy and uncomfortable, she had asked my son-in-law to accompany her for the feed. There was to be no respite, though. Again, there was the whispering – only this time, *he'd heard it too*.

It totally freaked out the both of them when we, yet again, assured them it hadn't been us.


So, who *was* it?

What could possibly be going on in such a new building? I knew the previous owners had lived there for many years, and they had all been very much alive when they'd left – and prior to them, it had been a long-term rental to another family from the village.

There is one possible clue, and it *is* only a maybe – as I can find no documented evidence to back up the claim that it had ever definitely happened.

A few months after the visit – whilst chatting to our

neighbour – the subject of the previous owners had once again come up in conversation. However, this time, she let slip a nugget of information that could change everything.

'You know about that French lad, I guess?'

'French lad? ...No'

'The one they'd had staying with them?'

When I again shook my head – she had gone on to fill me in on the details.

My predecessors, the previous owners, had once had a young French student staying. A young man who had been helping look after the kids – while they were away at work. A kind of Au Pair, I guess you'd say.

What she told me next, though, was truly awful.

Apparently, he had been cycling down the steep and treacherous Mine Hill – heading towards the lower village – when the brakes on his bike had totally and catastrophically failed.

Unable to make the sharp bend at the bottom at such high speed – he had hit the wall hard, killing him instantly.

Could this then be the reason for the whispering? Could it be why my daughter and her husband had been the ones to hear it – and not me? After all, *they* had been speaking French to each other, hadn't they?

As I said, to this day, I have no absolute proof of this – but see no reason to doubt their story. It had come out of the blue – and it's not as if we'd been talking about ghosts or anything. It had just been a normal, matter-of-fact conversation – and besides, I have since heard this same sad tale from another separate source.

As it turned out though, I was, soon enough, to have an experience of my own in this house – and one that would really throw me.

It was still early morning, and I was lying in bed with my back to the door. My husband starts work at ridiculous o'clock, and he'd long since left for the daily grind.

Anyway – I lay on my side, eyes closed, just relaxing, and not thinking of anything in particular – just content that all was well with the world.

'Hi.'

The soft, mournful voice jolted through me.

I jumped up, startled by the unexpected sound of my husband's voice. Why was he here? What was wrong? Why did he sound so sad?

The questions flew thick and fast, one after the other through my head, as I twisted around quickly – jerking my head towards the door.

It was closed and he wasn't there!

But I had plainly heard him – he'd been right behind

me – in the room and, moreover... he'd sounded so strange, sad – somehow depressed.

Positive now that something was very wrong, I got straight on the phone and left him message after message.

'Ring me! As soon as you get this... Ring me!'

I'm sure he thought I'd gone quite mad – when he eventually got back to me during his first break of the morning.

No, he was fine. All was good – there was NO problem.

I hung up the phone, relieved.

But what the hell had I heard then?

I know it sounds crazy – and it was just one word – but I know my husband's voice – and that was *his* voice. But it wasn't just that – it was the depth of emotion that had somehow been squeezed into that one little word...

Now I have long since come to realise that spirit can and will mimic the voices of our loved ones.

Could this perhaps have been that same spirit? The one that my daughter had heard? If so, then maybe it had just been trying to communicate with me, in a way that it knew would get my attention?

If so, it had certainly worked – it *got* my attention!

It's just so very frustrating, though, not knowing exactly what they want and what they need from me.

But mine is not to reason why...

Chapter 12
# So... You Still Want To Investigate?

So... you've tried out an investigation, considered all the pitfalls, and it still hasn't put you off. On the contrary, you are now totally fired up and couldn't imagine a world where you'd never be able to investigate again. *Welcome to my world*!

So, what are you going to do now?

Take up investigating on a small scale and just visit neighbourhood sites during the day? Join a local team? – Or maybe even start a team of your own?

To help you in your deliberations, here is a quick run-through of a few of the options available to you, and I've added some of the pros and cons of each.

**The Lone Investigator**

There are many advantages to going it alone and forsaking the company of other like-minded nutters – but there are just as many downsides.

One significant bonus, however, is that you will definitely not have to put up with any trust issues or in-fighting ...unless, of course, you start doubting your own eyes and ears, and take yourself to task over it!

Another huge tick, is that if there's no one else there with you, then any potential evidence gained must surely be all the more credible.

It's true – you'll get to choose where and when you go – with no interference or pressure from others. But you MUST take extra care with your safety.

Plan ahead and always make sure that someone knows exactly where you are and, more to the point – at what time they are to panic, and run around like a headless chicken, in the event of your continued unexplained absence.

Being a lone investigator can work well for someone that is content with public access sites and cheaper hire venues – but the cost would almost certainly prohibit any of the better-known haunted locations. Hire costs alone for these places, can be eye-watering.

Always respect private property if you're out and about exploring suitable investigation sites. It may appear derelict and unloved to you, but it will belong to someone. Track down the owners and seek permission – and yes, they probably *will* turn you down, but that is their right – and you must respect it.

**Join A Team**

Finding a position in a suitable team can be hard going.

If a team runs efficiently, then most will be quite content to stay as they are and won't be looking for new members. *(If it ain't broke, don't fix it!)*

Others, though, have a habit of taking on more and more people and, although it's just my opinion, will quickly become too large to work efficiently as a team.

You will soon realise that there are many types of paranormal groups, too – the science-based, the spiritualistic, the sceptical...

The biggest difference of all though, is whether or not they are a commercial enterprise? As in, do they sell event tickets to the public – or just do their own private investigations?

As ever, of course, there are pros and cons to each.

The pros of joining a commercial team include regular access to some truly phenomenal sites. You will guide the public to get the best out of their visit – meeting many lovely people in the process.

The flip side, is that you will go to the same sites over and over – and they can, eventually, become repetitive and samey. You'll rarely be able to investigate properly, as you are really only there to help host others – and any evidence captured at the site may not be taken as seriously as it should be – and, in fact, may not even be followed up at all.

Non-commercial groups are usually the way to go, but as I said, it is hard to find an opening.

Make contact through social media, or via their website *(if they have one)*. Ask them to keep your details if they don't have an opening. Meet up with them if you get the chance – because it's really more about whether you could bond with the team, than anything else.

**Make A Team**

Creating a new paranormal team from scratch is hard work and a real labour of love – and don't let anyone convince you otherwise. It's not all about logos, black hoodies, and team baseball caps. There is just so much to consider.

First and foremost, you must be so careful *who* you take on.

It's vital that you can work well together, respecting each other's views and opinions – and that you both have the same long-term goal.

Take your time. People are not what they first appear to be, and trust is everything. All too often, teams fall apart as rivalries and petty jealousies take hold.

If you *are* going to be running a team, then you will need to be strong in setting firm boundaries and steadfast in upholding them.

Don't be in a rush to take on more people. Smaller is definitely better.

Do you want a more scientific team, or one more on the spiritual side? Often, the two don't mix. Mediums can greatly help an investigation – being versed in protection, communication and helping send spirits over – but is this what you want?

Equipment will always be one of the most significant ongoing expenses of running a team, and most will have a least one decent night vision camera – probably a range of EMF Meters and some other assorted gadgets – such as a Spirit Box, Laser Grids or Beam Barriers.

Bear in mind that any equipment that needs to be plugged into the mains during an investigation, will need to have a current PAT Testing certificate.

Equipment may be right up there on the costs stake – but right at the top, without a doubt, will be the cost of hiring venues. Some of these places are literally thousands and well outside the reach of smaller teams, for sure.

Ensure that all team members can and do, pay their share.

Having people with extremes of income ranges within the same team can cause big problems in itself – so make sure everyone joining knows roughly what will be expected of them.

Outside public access investigations are always a possibility. There are countless ancient sites, derelict chapels, stone circles, cairns and the like – but again, always make sure that you have permission to be there *(whenever necessary)*.

You might be tempted to advertise for access to private, reputedly haunted homes – but here, I have to advise caution.

So, someone has contacted you, saying their house is haunted and that they need you to come and help – but BEWARE.

You don't know who they are. You don't know if they are mentally stable. You don't know if you'll end up making matters a hundred times worse, should you happen to agree with them that their home *is* haunted! You could literally end up with a tragedy on your hands.

I have never done it – and I would strongly recommend that you don't consider it either.

To add to your woes on the cost front, you will need full public liability insurance. A must for any team that intends to hire a venue – but it can also cover team injury and equipment if required. Each team member will need to be named individually on the policy.

A well-thought-out team dynamic will include people that thrive on the technical side of investigating – those that love setting up equipment, running base-line tests and monitoring things throughout the investigation. And then you'll need someone that lives for evidence review – record keeping, or the taking of notes from people who may have witnessed phenomena.

To run a team well, people have to know precisely what is expected of them. All too many want to turn up for the investigation, but will have NO interest in helping get venues, setting up equipment or trawling through hours of footage to spot potential captures.

Finally, there is the documentation needed by certain larger venues. Many will require you to complete a risk analysis form and present it, together with the team insurance policy, prior to commencing any investigation.

Ah, it's a fun life, eh?


Whichever path you take to begin investigating, you'll need to think carefully about networking and the use of social media – and choose whether you even want to go down that route in the first place. Most in the paranormal field don't work totally alone. They feed off each other, support each other and learn from each other.

The buzzword of the paranormal community is *'paraunity'*. It's not always adhered to, it's true – and there's always been way too much backstabbing and inter-team jealousies. But if you can swing it, working together can literally open doors for you. It can get you into places that you wouldn't have dreamed possible.

By sharing larger venues between teams, you can slash your costs and save enough money to allow you to investigate more often.

You'll be able to share and discuss any evidence you caught and have the opportunity to gain valuable insight and perspective.

You can ask for advice on equipment and the best place to buy it – as well as get guidance on potential future investigation sites.

Yes, social media can drive you nuts – but sometimes, occasionally, it's simply worth the pain.

## Chapter 13
# Footsteps
My Paranormal Experiences...

One of the all-time greats in the way of paranormal phenomena, is experiencing the sound of unexplained footsteps – and when heard for the first time, the unmistakable clomp of heavy, solid steps, where *no one could possibly be*, is simply spine-tingling.

Many times, I have experienced what would seem to be two or three quick steps – but there have been a few occasions when it has been more.

Oh, *so much* more.

Remember those footsteps that had first climbed, and then descended the stairs of my French farmhouse? Yes, a classic example of what I'm talking about! But another similar occasion that will always remain embedded in my mind, was whilst the team were away investigating – in deepest, darkest, and not so dangerous Devon.

Our location for that night was a remarkable, fully restored Tudor building dating from the Elizabethan era and located in the very heart of the historic town of Totnes.

The part-timbered four-storey structure was originally built way back in 1575 – and had been both home, and place of business, to a prominent and prosperous local cloth merchant.

In more recent times, having been comprehensively restored by the local council, it was now in use as the Totnes Museum and, amongst its many other treasures, was a substantial wooden loom, a section devoted to the history of textiles, and numerous examples of fine Elizabethan furnishings.

Gracing us with their silent presence that night too – and outnumbering us at least four to one – were a select group of elegantly posed mannequins, busily *not* going about their day-to-day tasks. *Thank you, God!*

Renowned in the area for being haunted – for some reason, on this occasion, I'd thought it appropriate to take a squiz at previously reported phenomena – just in case anything comparable should happen during the night. Though to be frank, this is not my customary habit. More typically, I prefer to leave that sort of research until after my visit.

So, what did I find? What might we expect from the

night – always supposing we were to come across similar?

First and foremost – there was the reported sighting of an angry man. *Yeah... That's one for the lads.*

The apparent repeated sightings of a phantom cat ...*I'll take that one!*

And then there was the presence of the ghost children – notably a small boy and girl ...*Hmmm, yeah – the jury's still out on that one!*

Most peculiar of all, though – bizarrely – was people reporting a sudden feeling of seasickness – of nausea whilst on the stairs. The reason behind this oddity? Thought to be because the central post of the spiral stairway had been made from an old ship's mast. Certainly unusual.

So then – onto the investigation.

We had decided during the initial walk around that we'd concentrate our efforts on the two uppermost floors, rather than attempt to spread ourselves too thin. Somehow, they'd felt the more active – spiky*!*

We'd started the night however, with a brief investigation of the lower levels – which included a stunning example of a medieval kitchen – and that loom! Wow!

I would have loved to be able to spend more time in the loom room – I feel it has a story to tell. That night though, I simply believed that the higher levels would yield more results.

So now, setting up upstairs, we'd whittled down the choices again and opted to place the locked-off night vision camera on the landing of the topmost floor – where we would also start the investigation proper.

Now, before I forget... *those stairs*...

Having now had the chance to check them out for myself, several times – both up and down. I don't doubt that visitors reported feeling queasy – it had done the same for me. Although to be a total killjoy, I reasoned the strange nauseating effect was most likely caused by the wonkiness of the steps themselves.

But then, that's the great thing about investigating, isn't it?

Sometimes it's as much about finding a natural cause for an occurrence, as it is a supernatural one.

So – back to business and a few hours into the investigation. Activity-wise, it wasn't the most thrilling of starts. Those attempting glass divination had found it extremely hard going, although it ultimately picked up pace. Responses to our questions seemed to suggest that we were in contact with a young girl – who then confirmed the presence of another, more reticent spirit.

During that session, two of the team simultaneously saw a tall, dark shadow – a mass, hovering within the open doorway, whilst a third had sensed its presence but hadn't actually *seen* anything.

Could this be the spirit that the girl had spoken of?

Maybe, it would tie in.

Unfortunately – I didn't see or sense *anything* myself at that time – *not even the cat! (Heavy sigh)*, so have nothing of use to add.

With the night now drawing on, we left the camera where it was and quickly moved down a level – to settle ourselves in the third-floor front parlour, where we found ourselves now surrounded by period Elizabethan furnishings – and a couple more of those well-dressed mannequins *(well – they were dressed a lot better than us, for sure!)*.

We had already been there some forty minutes and, as yet were still totally unsuccessful in our attempt to incite spirit to do something, *anything*!

About to call it a night – suddenly, a chair scraped noisily across the bare wooden floorboards behind us.

Startled, we performed an instant 180 – its sudden brief loudness seeming thunderous to our ears against the previous silence of the building.

The chair in question, was now halfway under the writing desk, on the other side of the room to where we were now all stood – in a line, facing it.

Finally ...*YES!*

We were still very much concentrating on that chair,

when abruptly and as one, our heads shot up, at the sound of loud, clear footsteps ringing out from above us.

Comically, all four of us silently followed its progress with eyes wide and mouths open – as they tracked clear across the empty room above.

Breaking our trance, we shot out of the room and up those stairs *(yes, we can be brave ...sometimes)*.

We were literally seconds in getting up there but found nothing and no one.

A later review of the footage shot that night, revealed that both camera and recorder had clearly picked up our reactions to the steps. We could hear our excited exclamations and the noise of our own steps, loud on the wooden treads as we'd chased up the stairs. But of the original footsteps? There was not a peep.

Four of us had clearly heard it, yet it wasn't on the recordings.

Hmmm, no evidence to show.

How unusual! (Cue sarcastic roll of the eye.)

It certainly made it into my top-twenty of memories, though, if only *(sadly)* for the fact that it had made *me* run.


Even higher in my chart of paranormal goings-on, though, was an experience that made two seasoned paranormal investigators literally shriek and hug each other. Yes, I will admit it! – I shrieked. Not a scream, though *(Definitely not a scream!)*.

I remember it well. I mean... how could I really forget?

I was in the Officers Mess of an old RAF airfield complex. Operational between 1942 and 1945 – it now forms a part of the Davidstow Airfield and Cornwall at War Museum – and can be found near Camelford in North Cornwall. In a room literally crammed full of mannequins, dressed in various wartime costumes, and posed as though mingling for a party. *(Are you sensing a theme here?)*

Most of the others had just left, for the inevitable fag break and being the only two in the team that didn't smoke, my partner in crime and I, had opted to stay put and carry on with what we were doing. The chance to grab a much smaller, more intimate style of investigation was just too good an opportunity to pass up.

Well, we parked our sorry carcasses on a bench by the double doors – at the end of that large, mannequin-filled expanse of pitch-black room. The high arch of the corrugated roof made an occasional ticking sound as it cooled in the night air, but apart from that, there was silence. Thick and heavy.

'Is there anyone with us?'

What was that?

A light scuffling from the furthest reaches of the room caught our attention. *Was something moving?*

'If anyone is here with us now, please step forward – come towards us.'

Whose bloody bright idea was that? (Actually – I guess I'll have to admit that it was mine).

Anyway, it came.

It came FAST!

That almost insignificant bit of scuffling, had quickly turned into the sound of loud running footsteps – and it was coming right at us!

Well, I'm not ashamed to admit it – we panicked.

We acted instinctively and shrieked – grabbed at each other, and quickly turned on the torch, pointing it into the blackness.

The footsteps stopped dead and *(of course)*, you guessed it – there was nothing to see.

Nothing!

## Chapter 14
# Equipment
The Paranormal Technological Boom...

I swear, every day brings more and more supposed paranormal equipment onto the market. All carefully packaged, marketed, and aimed at less experienced investigators or those just starting up – and sold as the next wonder item that you simply must have!

But what is behind this boom?

Money – pure and simple.

The ongoing popularity of the paranormal is bringing a whole new generation of would-be investigators into the field. Inspired by a glut of ghost hunting programmes – they long to follow in their hero's footsteps and venture out into the night, armed to the teeth with the latest gadgets.

I have no problem with this. Why would I, when young

blood can bring fresh excitement into the paranormal world - but what I do have a problem with – is rip-off merchants taking advantage of unsuspecting people.

The profit potential when successfully marketing a new piece of equipment is huge. Knock a weirdly shaped gothicky-looking box up using a 3D printer, fill it with some impressive wiring obtained from the Pound Shop, give it a suitably spooky sounding name and bingo! An absolute bargain at a tenth the price!

Yeah, it will probably fall apart after the first use – but that's only because of the extreme spirit activity it helped provoke ...*right?*

I have myself tested the claims of some of these offerings – and yes, some of them do seem to work as claimed – but think logically. Do you *really* need a movement detector that can pick up any movement within a five-meter radius – even when on the other side of a solid wall? I mean, if something sets it off – how will you know what it might have been? It's in another room, right? Yes, it could be that spirit that you're sure is haunting the place – or it could just be an inquisitive mouse!

Don't get me wrong, there *is* a place for equipment – but you need to be selective and not be taken in by the claims of unscrupulous sellers. Look hard at the build quality and take good note of reviews. Check prices carefully too, before you commit. The fact that it is selling for £5000 doesn't actually mean that it is worth it ...or even that it will work!

Most equipment used by investigators will be affected by phone signals and electrical appliances. Make sure they are suitably isolated by turning everything off and always switching your mobile to flight mode.

Keep detectors away from potential rodent runs and bug-infested areas – and shield them from gusts of wind, water droplets and excess dust. All of these can affect your results.

So – let's run through some kit items regularly seen on investigations.

Some are better than others, for sure. Some I use regularly and others are simply not for me. Other investigators, however, may swear by a gadget that I simply don't like. I will give you my opinion on each – but remember, it's just that, an opinion.

**Night Vision Cameras**

A good night vision camcorder can be a great asset. They will allow you to see through the darkness and turn night into day. However, a good one will set you back many hundreds – so you'll need to balance cost against value. If you are not prepared to sift through hours of footage – in great detail to spot any potential evidence, then I would suggest there is no point in making that investment.

When investing in a camera – be sure that it has night vision capability, or can work in extremely low light, by checking the LUX value. *(LUX is the scale describing how much light the camera requires to 'see.')* For example: 0.1 lux would be roughly equivalent to the light cast by a quarter moon.

When you get down to light levels this low, however, you will need a good infrared light to really make things clear. Night vision camcorders do come with their own built-in IR lighting – but personally, I have always found it insufficient – preferring to use additional external infrared lighting as well.

My personal choice of camera is the Panasonic HC-VXF990, used with Sony HVL-IRM infrared lighting – but there are many great models out there.

**CCTV**

Hmmm, do you really need CCTV? – Probably not!

A night vision CCTV set is a fantastic piece of kit – *if you're really going to go for it* – but be warned – if you choose a set with, say, eight cameras – then you'll have eight times the amount of footage to check through. It could translate to literally *days* of trawling.

You'll also need to consider the time and effort necessary to set it up in the first place.

I guess, unless you're a filmmaker, its best use would probably just be to set it up and to have someone sit at the monitor – watching for anomalies in real time.

**Thermal Imagers**

This is an interesting bit of kit, for sure.

If you purchase a stand-alone model, they could set you back thousands – but a much better idea is to buy an attachment for your phone. Flir produce some excellent models and are available in either IOS or Android with USB-C or Micro-USB connectivity.

They cost around the mid-two hundreds – but you could always consider buying used.

One especially useful feature is its dual camera capability. One lens uses normal light, whilst the other 'sees' in heat, and the two are overlaid on the screen.

This opens up a fascinating new version of the world around you – bringing it to life before your very eyes. *Now you are seeing the thermal world.*

How is this useful in the field of paranormal investigating, though? I hear you ask.

Well, just imagine, if you will – a situation where you were to catch sight of a moving human figure on the screen. You can't see anything yourself, but that may just be because it's too dark, right? Now – suppose that figure was purple in colour – denoting an object considerably colder than its environmental surroundings.

Any *living* entity would have clearly shown up in the brightest of colours – predominantly whites and pale yellows.

Now *that* would be awesome, wouldn't it?

Added to its worth, is being able to use either the phone's camera or video mode. Doing something as simple as a walk-through, while using the Flir to video – could bring a whole new level to your investigation.

## Full Spectrum Cameras

A full spectrum camera is basically one that is able to *see*, using a much greater range of light wavelengths than is normal.

Often, hand converted from older style point and click digital cameras – they won't give you a 'normal' picture, as the colour will be distorted by the presence of ultraviolet and infrared light – but they can give fascinating results.

I have seen some remarkable images over the years, some of which have become real talking points. One particularly awesome example, taken by a friend, was the partially transparent image of a lady, with downturned face – snapped during a daytime visit at a favourite stately home.

If you can manage to get hold of a decent one without too much outlay then I would certainly recommend adding it to your kit.

When it comes to taking photos in the hope of getting potential paranormal evidence, though – may I offer one bit of advice?

Always take your photos in sets of 3.

That way, should an anomaly show up in one of your pictures, you will have others, taken from the same perspective with which to compare it. This applies equally to both full spectrum and standard cameras.

**Digital Voice Recorders**

In my humble opinion, a good quality voice recorder is a must-have piece of equipment, and they can be used in many ways on an investigation. In the background as a control – left in locked off rooms to help cover larger venues – or to try EVP *(Electronic Voice Phenomenon)* burst sessions – during which you ask your questions, then stay absolutely still and silent to see if any *(otherwise unheard)* response is picked up on the recording.

Before recording – go right through the settings and configure it for optimum use. Make sure the mic is set to 'sensitive' and that the recording quality is 'high' *(always use the highest possible)*. Poor quality recordings can lead to sound distortion – which in turn, could be misinterpreted as something paranormal.

Everyone must remain silent and perfectly still when using the recorder to ask questions. Never move your fingers or hand while holding the device, and keep it away from clothing etc. The rustle of a coat sleeve, for example, can easily be misinterpreted as something more sinister.

If an unexpected noise is heard, make sure you log it – just say, 'distant car –my stomach,' or the like.

My personal preference when it comes to recorders, is the Olympus DM-670. It has superb sound quality and is light and easy to use.

## EMF Meters

The range of EMF Meters available these days can be boggling, and prices are just as many and varied, but do you even need one?

EMF Meters simply read changes to localised electromagnetic fields. The theory being that the presence of spirit can affect these readings – or... that spirit are able to create EMF themselves – thereby influencing the meter and so bringing about a form of communication. Either way, I believe yes – they have a place.

The one you are most likely to come across is the **KII**. A small hand-held device that features five coloured lights, ranging from green to red, that works quite simply – the more lights showing – the stronger the field being read.

These are readily available and quite cheap – but personally, I wouldn't touch them. They are far too prone to everyday interference, like electrical outlets and hidden wiring – and can even be set off just by moving your hand too quickly.

They are too easily influenced for me – and I have known people manipulate them by touching the buttons of a phone, hidden within their pocket.

A much better bet, in my eyes, is the **Trifield** or its later incarnation, the **Trifield II**. Featuring a needle dial, it can be set to read electric, magnetic or both simultaneously – and features a small red light and audible tone that will mark any significant changes in atmospherics.

For best use, this one really needs to be stationary – but it is very stable and stands well on its own.

The **Rem Pod** is our next paranormal offering – with its unusual and distinctive looks. A round drum-shaped device with four different coloured lights, equally spaced around the top, and a central extendable aerial.

The major difference between the Rem Pod and the previous items, is that the Rem Pod emits its own electromagnetic field – rather than just measuring changes in surrounding EMF.

If this field is broken – by something getting too close to the aerial, the various colours will light, and an audible tone will be heard – again, depending on the strength of the interference.

These days, EMF meters will often be placed within everyday objects – in an effort to trigger communication. Most commonly, you'll find them in toys, most notably **EMF Bears**.

The simple idea behind this is that the bear could attract, say, a child spirit – and will light up if touched or affected by a strong change in EMF.

They have limited use, but if you are ever anywhere that is said to have child spirits... then why not?

What's my favourite, though? I hear you ask. The answer is simple in this case – it's the **MEL/REM 8704R**. A four-in-one meter that is a torch, Rem Pod, EMF Meter and temperature gauge – all in one easy-to-hold device.

## Spirit Box

My thoughts on the spirit boxes are many and varied.

I hate them – yet can't deny that I have had some outstanding results using them. But first of all, what is it?

A Spirit Box is a device that will scan rapidly through radio channels, without stopping – in either a forward or backward direction and resulting in tiny snatches of noise from each. The idea is that if you hear a complete sentence *(preferably one that ties in with whatever you've just asked)*, it must be of significance. As no one channel is on longer than a split second – you *should* hear no complete sentences.

Spirit boxes go by too many names to list, and are often hand-produced items, ranging in price from £60, to well into the £1000s ...though *please*, never even consider those. They all do the same essential task.

One of the better-known spirit boxes has to be the SB7, and its later incarnation, the SB11. It is reasonable enough in price and works okay, but oh, the noise! I hate it! To me, it's reminiscent of an old train on a track. To be fair, though, many others swear by it. Just be prepared...

My favourite *(if such a thing exists in this case)*, is a converted **Radioshack 12-587**, although sadly – the radio itself is now discontinued, so it's getting harder and harder to obtain a good one.

Perhaps the most exciting spirit box that I have owned, would have to be the **Poltercom**. With a very Jules Verne, Steampunk-inspired outer shell, created by a 3D printer – it features a dial that clicks around as the radio scans through the channels.

Yes, I've had some good results from it – *but oh, the style!*

## Ovilus

A small device containing a database of thousands of words – that is said to react to changes within the electromagnetic field and select words accordingly.

The theory is quite simple – if spirits can affect EMF, then they may be able to manipulate the Ovilus into selecting and speaking certain words.

I don't know. Unfortunately, as yet, I've not had an opportunity to fully test one – and unless you're willing to fork out over £500 on an item that, after all, is known to have words pre-programmed into it – then I would suggest crossing that one firmly off the list.

## EMF Pumps

If ghosts are able to manipulate electromagnetic fields, could they also be attracted by them? Does pumping EMF into the atmosphere increase paranormal activity?

This is what these pumps are all about. Creating the right conditions. To be honest, though, I've never had much to do with them. For one thing, I can't stand the noise they create whilst working.

**Beam Barriers**

A standard home security device that has been appropriated for paranormal investigation. Primarily used in doorways, hallways or on stairs – they will emit an audible tone if someone *(or, hopefully something)* breaks the beam.

These are just a handful of the countless devices put out there as the next must-have item for your paranormal equipment collection. But honestly, you *really* don't need to spend a fortune.

Now to get real – and give you a few ideas for investigative tools that don't cost the Earth. In fact, many of them cost nothing at all – they'll be items that you, most likely, already have in your home.

**Automatic writing** - All you'll need is a pen, plain paper and maybe something to rest it on.

**Dowsing Rods** - Not typically expensive anyway – but why not make your own? You'll just need two thin metal rods, bent in a right angle.

**Pendulums** - A simple crystal hung on a short chain

that is possible to pick up for under a fiver – but again, you could always fashion your own.

**Torch** - If you have a torch with a slide type on/off button, it could be used by turning the switch *almost* on – and by asking spirit to turn it on for you. I have seen this work.

**Trigger Objects** - These could be almost anything – the only limit here is your imagination. Coins, small toys, an old bullet, symbols… Just try to find something that would be relevant for wherever you are planning to investigate.

They can be set out and photographed – or maybe drawn around. The object of the exercise? To simply to see if they have been moved at the end of the night.

**Flour** - *No, I haven't flipped out!* Flour can be used to show if something has been interfered with or moved. Just don't spread it across the floor of that beautiful historic building, eh.

**Laser Pen** - Not free – but again, it's possible to pick one up very cheaply.

Finally, the best investigative tool of all…

**Your body, your eyes, and your ears** – Take note of how your body is reacting. Have you got a sudden attack of the goosebumps for no apparent reason? Or maybe a feeling of dread …or of being watched?

If so, learn to trust your instincts.

· · ·

At a push, though, all you really need, is your mobile *(on flight mode)*, a torch and your enthusiasm. The mobile can be used for still shots, filming, taking notes, and EVP recording.

So don't let a lack of funds keep you from following your dreams.

## Chapter 15
# The Shadow Man
My Paranormal Experiences...



Let's go back to the beginning – back to my shadow man...

Did you *really* think you were going to get away without hearing about this one? In infinite detail? If so, you obviously don't know me well enough yet.

Let's recap...

It was 2:15 am on a cold March morning in 2013. Me, my daughter, and her best friend, were lucky enough to be taking part in a public night paranormal investigation – at the infamous Bodmin Jail in my beloved North Cornwall.

It had been a great evening, and active too – but energies were starting to flag now, and activity had dropped considerably.

Tired – but not ready yet to call it a night, we'd wearily

trudged into the Long Room, the ground floor level of the derelict prisons' civil wing – hoping that the table that had been left there, would finally be free.

Sadly, it was not to be – and yet again, it was in use.

Luckily this time though, the three women present were very accommodating – kindly inviting us to join them in their table tipping session. They had been attempting, as yet unsuccessfully, to make contact – and you never know – maybe our presence would help.

The three of us squeezed in – placing our fingertips on the tabletop as they agreeably shuffled round to allow us room. I remember being distinctly unimpressed though, when they'd unexpectedly upped the ante – and had started singing nursery rhymes, in a curious attempt to draw in the jail's child spirits.

This really wasn't my thing – but I didn't want to appear rude when they been so welcoming. Deciding to stick it out, I kept my fingers on the still motionless table – idly looking around the dark and shadowed room to the pitch-black cells beyond.

And that is when I saw him.

Silhouetted by the soft light of our base room, he strode in through the open doorway and immediately cut straight across to my right. Moving fast – his arms swinging with each gigantic step.

As I stared, my mind was a whirl. *Who was he?* I

hadn't spotted anyone in the group that night that was remotely near that size.

He was solid black to my eye – and even in the darkness of the unlit cell room, he was darker – much darker! Pure black. Not a feature to be seen.

Perplexed, I turned my head to follow his progress – my mind barely aware now of the touch of the table – or of the singing.

Away from the soft light of the doorway, he was getting harder to see.

Still striding – he passed in front of the locked off night vision camera with its single infrared light attachment (its little circle of red dots) – blocking it out entirely as he went. And as you now already know – when he reached the furthest, darkest corner of that godforsaken place, he just disappeared.

It wasn't an instant disappearance. It was as though he had just become one with the shadows of the room. He'd faded out.

My daughter and I exchanged glances – and as our eyes met, she raised her eyebrows in query. *She had seen him too!*

Noticing our distraction – the women faltered and stopped singing.

'What's the matter?'

'Have you seen something?' They turned from my daughter now – eagerly back to me.

'Yes...' We both related exactly what we had seen, about how dark he had appeared, and how *large*.

By now though, the ladies had already come up with their own theory.

Surely, it must have been Elizabeth? – the spirit woman that allegedly protects the younger inmates of the jail – the children and that she must have been drawn to towards us because of their singing.

This was no woman though. Absolutely no doubt about it.

So, who do I think he is?

I have thought on this long and hard and have only been able to reach one logical conclusion. I believe that he may have been a guard or overseer. He was Obviously no prisoner or at least, if he was then he'd been placed in a position of authority over the others. This was a big, strong, and confident man, striding with purpose. Owning his place

Weirdly – confirmation of our sighting was to come, some two years later, and under the strangest of circumstances.

I had been invited to the jail by a fellow investigator who was in the midst of making a new paranormal documentary series. The jail was next in his filming schedule, and as I was familiar with the place, he'd asked me along.

He is known for the peculiar and fascinating talent of

being able to produce EVPs on demand – and on virtually *every* attempt. A feat which I've not known anyone else be able to match – although I'm pretty confident, if there's one there must surely be others.

Anyway, we were at the jail, and I was hanging back, just observing, as the crew scurried about, busy setting up the necessary equipment and filming for B-roll shots. When unexpectedly, I heard someone yelling for me, from the lower floor hallway.

'*Hey* – Allison... come quick!'

What the hell?

I hurried down the steep granite stairway to find a long-term Facebook friend and member of the team, standing outside the entrance to the Long Room – hands clenched, as she peered anxiously around the corner.

'I've just seen someone... a man – in there.' She nodded towards the dark and dingy cell block. 'But... there's no one *there*?'

'Tell me exactly what you saw?'

I already had an inkling of what was to come, though. I could feel the hair rising on the nape of my neck,

'I saw a tall man – walking fast. He went across there,' she indicated the Long Room with her hand. 'But I don't know where he went. He just *disappeared*.'

'Okay...' This was bloody *awesome*. 'What did he look like? Can you describe him for me?'

'No, not really – he was pitch black.'

Needless to say, we were beyond excited at this point as we hurriedly compared notes. Two and a half years apart – viewed from an entirely different angle and at a different time of day. There was now bright summer sunshine outside, instead of the darkness of that cold distant night ...but it *was* him. The same man. Walking that exact same path. It was almost beyond belief.

Grinning ridiculously, we hastened to the control room, eager to check the night vision CCTV that was constantly in operation in that area.

Time and again we requested it be rewound, as we peered closely at the monitor – searching for anything that might confirm the sighting. But there was nothing. Not so much as an orb.

Having finally to admit defeat *(on the video front at least)*, the two of us shot off to tell the others – prattling excitedly as we went.

'Whoa... calm down. Just tell me exactly what happened.'

Well – we recounted our tales – hers and mine. I remember the amused scepticism on his face. Yes – he probably thought that we were just imagining things – but then... he had that talent ...didn't he?

What happened next, will always blow my mind.

He took the recorder out of his pocket and held up his hand for quiet.

'Let's ask the Spirits, shall we?' And diverting his attention to the task at hand, he asked *that* question.

'What did the ladies see? Was it a ghost, was it a spirit ...or have they just got over excited?'

Pressing record, he waited silently, for ten or so agonisingly long seconds – and on playback? *Yes* – there it was... an unmistakable whispery little voice and the answer was clear.

'It was a ghost.'

So – there you have it. Thanks to the unique skill of this very talented man, I've now had the fact that I had seen a 'ghost' *(a shadow of what has been before – a replay, unaware of our presence)* – confirmed by a 'spirit.' *(An intelligent entity that is aware of us and the current situation.)*

Life surely just doesn't get any better than that!


Built of local granite by French prisoners of war in 1779, Bodmin Jail has stood the test of time. Even surviving an attempt to dynamite it after it fell into a state of disrepair – after having long since closed its doors as a prison.

Unfortunately, there's no possibility to investigate further now – as in recent years it has been converted into a stunning (*I grudgingly admit it*) four-star hotel. But I do have to wonder as I look on at its shining new facade, how well their guests will sleep at night.

The day it closed for renovations was a sad day indeed (*for me, at least*). Some of the most memorable paranormal experiences of my life have been whilst within its resilient, moss-covered walls. Memories I will treasure forever.

One such instance, was capturing the likeness of a spirit man peering down at me from the heights of the unreachable derelict cells up above.

It was the early hours of a freezing February morning – and as I'd stood in the then derelict, roofless hulk of the naval wing, I was somehow *drawn* into raising my little point and snap camera towards the upper levels and taking the photo.

The following day on uploading the images to my computer, I instantly spotted him. White in colour against the grey green of the stained lichen-covered walls. Dark eyes, receding hairline... he was hunched forward, with what appeared to be a blanket wrapped around his shoulders – and he was looking right at me.

Another much later experience and one to make my all-time top ten, was when I'd been firmly pushed on my upper back. I'd been standing, silently keeping watch over a group of people currently going through the protection exercise at the start of their night's investigation.

Of course, I was startled, and had cried out – taking two quick steps forward to prevent myself from falling.

I glanced behind me swiftly – but there was no one there to see and grinning into the darkness, I silently mouthed, '*Thank you.*'

Hell, that was *GREAT*!

When I turned back around, however, twenty or more faces had all given up on their attempts to meditate and were looking at me expectantly.

'Sorry,' I muttered sheepishly, '...I was pushed.'

Their incredulity was plain to see on their faces though... obviously, I had just been pulling a stunt! Hadn't I?

I just wanted to go through the floor at that moment, as I saw the doubt and disbelief in their eyes.

Pushed? ...Yeah, *right*!

## Chapter 16
# Frequency

Yet More Musings...

When I think about the paranormal of all those ghostly goings on in the everyday world around us, I think of it as being akin to a *frequency*.

That's all well and good I hear you cry but what do you *mean* by frequency?

At its most basic, frequency is the number of sound waves that pass any fixed point, within a given amount of time. Low numbers of waves will amount to a low-frequency sound – and vice versa.

Now, I'm not saying that paranormal activity comes in the form of soundwaves *(although, who knows... it just might)*, but simply that it behaves in a similar way and that if you're going to experience it *(even if merely to sense its existence)* then you're going to need to be *tuned in*.

Have you ever considered why some people have seen ghosts while others have not? Or thought about why some can have regular paranormal experiences – yet others never will?

I have, it's a fundamental question – and one that I have found myself pondering many times over the years.

Why does paranormal activity happen to my daughter and me, whilst my son experiences none of it?

Why did my daughter and I both see the shadow man at the jail, when the four other women present that night saw nothing? Although, in the interest of telling the whole story here, I do have to add that two of the four had actually been facing in totally the wrong direction.

Why do mediums hear the voices of spirit when the rest of us hear only the babble of the living world? – the normalities of everyday life?

Why, why, why…?

It's undoubtedly one of life's great mysteries and the answer to which, I reason that none but an exceptional few could ever genuinely *know*. But I do have my *theories* on the subject.

Of course, she does…! (Cue sarcastic eye roll).

As I have already said, I am *no expert*. I don't even know if it's possible to *be* an expert. So – should you think I'm way off the mark – be kind.

I have previously shared my idea that the key to understanding the paranormal is to think about it in terms of energy. Paranormal energy exists. We may not see it, hear it or *feel* it – but it does exist – in much the same way that oxygen exists. We're not aware of it in any way *(well, apart from the fact that we're still alive, I guess)*, but it's definitely there.

But why can some sense that energy, while others cannot?

For that elusive answer, I now find myself leaning more and more towards the theory of 'frequency'.

Imagine, if you will, an old-style television ...one with the big old round dial – that you need to turn in order to find the next channel. Yes – I'm aware that you'll obviously never have used one of those but if you're unable to picture it in your mind, then an old radio will do just as well.

So, imagine starting to turn that dial. There is nothing on the screen, and nothing to hear just white noise.

Keep turning... so now you are starting to get something – just the faint crackle of a few broken words, interspersed with static ...just a little further. The words are clearer now and more discernible.

Another turn of the dial and *there*! You can hear the conversation entirely. And more just maybe there is now the flicker of a picture on the screen as well.

One final twist of that dial – and you can see and hear the broadcast you're fully tuned in!

So, this is what I believe it's like for people

experiencing the paranormal. You need to be tuned in – on the right level of consciousness.

If you are on level one and paranormal activity is taking place on level 4 – then you'll clearly experience none of it. It will all just go right over your head. Literally, it could all be kicking off around you.

The spirit of your great, great grandfather could be leaping up and down in front of you right now – going purple in sheer frustration, at you not heeding his advice about the unsuitability of your clothing. *'How could you possibly even consider wearing a skirt that short and when going out in public too!'*

Yet, you remain totally oblivious though probably happily so, with this particular example, if I'm honest but you get the picture.

If you want to have more awareness of our unseen world, then you'll need to find a way to raise your level of consciousness – to match that of the paranormal world around you to literally tune in.

But first, a word of caution...

Please carefully consider if that is what you really want. I mean maybe you won't want to hear that you're a lazy ne'er-do-well or that your clothes sense is a total embarrassment.

All jesting aside, though I'm going to assume now that you've already thought it through, and still have your mind firmly set on achieving at least some form of spiritual connection.

So, how are you going to do it?

One tried and tested method that you *could* use to bring about a change to your conscious state, is meditation. A technique designed to both bring about a heightened state of awareness, or explicitly focus your attention on a desired subject – and either way, it has a practical use within the paranormal field.

Meditation techniques are many and varied and due to its current popularity, detailed information is readily available online. So, with that in mind, I'm just going to skim over a few common themes, to start you on your way.

Methods that I have come across personally are:

- The visualising of a white light – which you can draw into yourself – letting it fill your body and overflow to create a cocoon of light around you. It's literally a way of bringing spiritual energy within – and will always feature prominently in a spiritual protection exercise.
- You could visualise your own special place *(your safe place)* in your mind. Allow your thoughts to mentally lead you on the journey that will take you there and from that point, it

may be easier for you to make contact with spirit.
- You could simply envisage a doorway, opening onto another realm. A quick and easy technique – if it will work for you.
- One particularly useful mental visualisation though, would be that of a lift. See yourself entering, the door closing softly behind you and then, in your mind's eye, selecting those buttons. This is powerful imagery to use – as it will enable you to easily imagine yourself, literally, going up through the various levels of consciousness.

But in all honesty, it really doesn't matter which method you use. Just choose whatever you think will work best for you. It's really more about the intent anyway. As ever – it's about '*getting in the zone*'.

Not everybody that sees phenomena on a regular basis will have to actively do this though – and I think it a safe bet, to say that mediums won't need it. So how can phenomena still happen to these people? How come *they* still get to have experiences?

Well – some people are just naturally on a higher plane than the rest of us. They were born that way – their mind functions just that little bit differently.

Other times, it could be that some external influence

has forced a temporary change to that person's usual level of consciousness and if a temporary shift of consciousness can happen to other people – then could we not somehow force a change on ourselves too?

I don't know that we could *force* one – but I do believe we can at least influence the possibility of a change – and of the many things that may help us do this, number one on the list would have to be your mood.

Believe it or not, your mood is a major influencing factor when it comes to connecting with the paranormal. And I am *not* talking about whether you are feeling 'spooky.' You know… that sudden scaredy feeling, usually accompanied by goosebumps and shivers, that you get when people around you start talking about ghosts and it's getting dark outside.

No – nothing to do with that. I mean your *actual* mood. Whether you are in a good place – happy, *on a high* – or whether you are down in the dumps and miserable?

I tend to think that like attracts like. If you are in a good place in your life – if you're happy and content – then you are more likely to connect with spirit in a positive way.

If, however, you are miserable, upset, or angry – you're going to unknowingly send out bad vibes, blocking connection with all that is good – but possibly still attracting things of a negative nature towards you.

I'm sure you're familiar with the phrases, to be in a *low mood* – or in *high spirits*? There is a direct correlation between these things. Make sure you pay attention to your state of mind it matters.

Something else that could bring about a temporary altered state, is the reliving of a strong memory from the past. Exploring that memory might take you back to experience once again *exactly* how you felt at that time – and if the feeling is strong enough it may be enough to help tune you in.

Keep in mind though, that your feelings can affect your mood. So be selective in your memory, and careful of what you dwell upon.

So, what of music as a means of altering your conscious state? Could that be used to heighten spiritual awareness?

Who among us could remain unaware of how much music affects our mood? Choosing that perfect piece of music could help you relax and could definitely assist in getting you into a meditative state.

It can take you back to a time long since passed – and therefore allow you the possibility of using it in a far more specific way.

Supposing you wanted to contact someone from your past. If you could bring to mind a particular song – a melody that had perhaps been playing when you had been together – then that same piece of music may be able to mentally take you back to that time.

Lose yourself in the music and you may, once again see their face in your mind's eye – the way that they turned their head – the sound of their voice and focusing like this, could just be enough to bring about a real spiritual connection.

At the very least, music remains a powerful medium and almost a form of self-hypnosis – that can help you create the right frame of mind and raise your level of consciousness.

There is, however, another possible way of temporarily altering your level of awareness. Though in truth, not a way that you could ever really have any control over. It's when you come into contact – purposefully or otherwise – with a place of power. When you walk into one of those earthly power points that I was speaking of. That stone circle – the haunted farmhouse – that quiet woodland glade…

These places will often do the job for you – automatically raising you into a heightened state of awareness.

In addition, storms and especially thunderstorms of an electrical nature could bring on a similar temporary upsurge.

Thunderstorms cause huge natural increases in localised energy. The air itself is charged with powerful electromagnetic energy, and lightning will either send this energy cloud to cloud, lighting the sky with blue-white flashes – or discharge it to Earth, in the form of a lightning bolt.

Doesn't it stand to reason that the presence of energy in such massive quantities, would cause a spike in localised paranormal activity and if so – why should it not do the same for you?

So, that storm, that has put a charge into the very air around you – just might, unknowingly, have notched you up a few levels internally too. Making you more receptive to the presence of spirit around you.

Nature is a wonderful thing.

If you have tried these methods, and ploughed through a few YouTube tutorials, but find yourself still unable to tune in under your own means – then I would suggest seeking a medium's help and advice. They may be able to tweak a technique – to make it right for you.

And if not then why not just let them do the work for you?

Let them make the contact – whilst you just sit back comfortably and wait for the results.

Chapter 17

# Apports - Little Presents From Beyond

My Paranormal Experiences...

There can surely be nothing stranger in this life than the receiving of an unexpected present a little gift from beyond.

It has happened several times in my life, and to be fair, it could have occurred on many more occasions – but the gift and its delivery is often subtle, and very easy to overlook. If your mind is elsewhere, on more pressing matters at the time of its receipt, you *may* spot it but probably wouldn't realise its significance.

These little gifts, these presents from the spirit world, are known as apports – and can happen anywhere and at any time.

An apport is basically the transference of an article from one place to another. Or the sudden appearance of a physical object from an unknown source produced by paranormal means and occasionally associated with poltergeist activity.

The first apport *(that I have been aware of at least)* was some five years ago now. It was early morning on my day off. Just a typical, run-of-the-mill day. Nothing special about it – and I had nothing of importance on my mind.

I was alone in the house and up in my room – pottering about, making the bed, tidying up and just getting ready for the day ahead.

Crossing the bedroom to the ensuite, I performed my ablutions without event. (*Well, thank goodness for that!*)

When I stepped back out of the room however, I stopped dead. My mouth forming an unvoiced 'oh'.

*There,* on the floor – were two shiny pennies.

Just outside the door and unmissable on the pale grey of the carpet.

I flopped onto the end of the bed, exhaling heavily still staring in wonder at the offending articles.

There was absolutely no way that they'd been there before.

Bending for a closer look, I picked them up, studying them in awe – but they were just regular shiny little penny pieces. Nothing out of the ordinary except for how they'd arrived, of course.

Placing them reverently on my bedside table, I looked around my room and, smiling, whispered, 'Thank you.'

Had they been sent to draw my attention? Or were they perhaps a gift? Either way where had they come from?

The only coins I kept in the house were in those little plastic bank bags – already counted out and ready to go to the post office – including some in a part filled bag that had a little note attached to say how much was in there. *Yes, I know... OCD or what! But that's just me.*

Could they maybe have taken them from there?

So, cue a frantic penny-checking session. Not only the part bag but the others too.

If spirit had taken these two pennies from my coin store, then I wanted to know about it. I counted and counted again. Nope, all was as it should be.

So, where the hell had they *come* from? It is one thing to have items moved from place to place within your house, but quite another to have them appear out of nowhere.

Exciting, though! *Very exciting.*


So, I told my husband – yeah, he probably just thought I'd gone nuts. I told my paranormal buddies – who were simply awestruck *(it's great having friends like that, isn't it?)*. The following day, I was sat at the dressing table, on the phone with my daughter in France – telling her!

I had just finished explaining what had happened –

and was literally mid-sentence, when I glanced down. There, at my feet, was another gleaming penny.

There was no noise – and nothing to announce its appearance.

Well, I guess you can imagine my excitement on that particular phone call.

Obviously, I spent the new few weeks with my eyes permanently glued to the floor – literally wherever I went. Nothing out of the ordinary was to appear though and after weeks passed, I put it to the back of my mind.

It was now December, and we were getting ready for the next house move. Everything was boxed and ready to go. All ornaments, trinkets, books and bits and bobs of every kind were packed neatly away in readiness for the removal men, who were due in just two days' time.

For some reason, that night I woke up in the early hours and there it was my next little present. Lit by the soft red glow of the LED clock on an otherwise empty bedside table – and literally *right next to me!*

A shiny silver sixpence!

Turning on the light, I picked it up and peered at it closely. It was shiny and looked almost new – but with just the tiniest of scratches on the right-hand side, just over the thistle.

*What the hell...?*

I mean, where does one even get a sixpence from?

I certainly didn't own one. Well... that's not exactly true anymore, is it? I guess I do now!

Taking it as a lucky charm, I determined to keep it close and, thanking my unseen benefactor, tucked it safely away in my purse.

And there it stayed my shiny little gift.

It accompanied me on my travels for many months, before one day, under yet more mysterious circumstances, vanishing again.

I don't know how, but it just wasn't there anymore. Realistically though, I reasoned that it had probably just fallen out of my purse at some stage, and its loss had gone unnoticed.

So, months have gone by, I am now living in my new place – and busy gathering together everything that I would need, in readiness for our upcoming holiday to France. A treat to celebrate our 20$^{th}$ wedding anniversary (*I did mention that my husband was long-suffering didn't I?*)

I was idly turning the ring on my finger, my wedding and engagement ring all rolled into one, while considering whether or not I should take it. What if I lost it?

I always take it off when I go to sleep. What if something were to happen if it were to fall off the bedside table or something and I didn't realise?

Ah, don't be so daft, woman! It'll be fine.

Anyway, I continued packing and thought no more of it. The next evening, we were due to catch the ferry and we would be on our way.

So, the following day comes. I get up, as usual, go to grab my ring from the bedside table and you guessed it, it wasn't there!

Unbelievable!

What the hell had I done with it?

I quickly checked my desk, the *only* other place that I ever usually kept it but of course, it wasn't there either – and from that point on, I went into overdrive proceeding to turn the house upside down.

I looked under sofas, under beds, pulled the bedding off, took seat cushions off and felt down the sides of chairs you name it – I looked under it, around it and over it! Deep down though, I knew I wouldn't find it. I'd already figured out that it wasn't there to find.

Part of me felt sick to the stomach that it had gone, whilst the other part was still quite confident that all would be fine.

So, the holiday came and went and it had been fantastic. Beautiful weather, relaxing sea views – spoilt rotten! Just what the doctor ordered. Unfortunately, as is always the way, it was over way too soon.

Back to the grind now and my fifth day back home.

I got up that morning (yes, alone - he that shall not

be named had, as usual, left for work many hours before) and went into the bathroom for my usual morning routine.

I opened the door to come back into my room, and there it was, my ring! Placed neatly on the corner of the dressing table, just inside the door where it definitely had *not* been, just five minutes before.

Well – I snatched it up and quickly rammed it onto my finger. Elated to have it back, and grinning from ear to ear, I thanked the spirits for looking after it and for returning it to me, of course.

I had already considered the possibility that they had taken it to prevent it from being lost overseas. Maybe, just possibly that had been on the cards to happen. But either way, I guess I'll never know.

What truly fascinates me, though... what keeps me awake if I start to think about it – is *where did it go?* And *how did they even do that?*

I have considered the possibility that it was just somehow shielded from my eyes. Kind of... made invisible to me. But obviously, that couldn't be the case. It was taken from my bedside table – but returned to the dressing table – across the room, and somewhere I have never kept it.

How is it even possible for an article to simply disappear – reappearing somewhere else at a later point in time?

Could it be somehow taken into another dimension?

I don't know.

It boggles the brain and these days, my brain is boggled quite enough!


So, I have since received one further little gift.

Just a few short months ago – two house moves and almost three years after its initial disappearance, there, on the windowsill of the ensuite, was my sixpence! The very same one with the tiny scratch to the right – just over the thistle.

Ah, it's a wonderful paranormal world we live in, isn't it?

But I have to wonder how long will I get to keep it *this* time?

## Chapter 18

# Staying Safe In Our Paranormal World

More of Those Pesky Hazards...

I'm guessing that personal safety probably isn't one of the first things on your mind, when you think about the world of paranormal investigation.

You just want to get out there, right? Crack your equipment case open and start bringing in that evidence.

But think on for a moment, for the virgin investigator, there are a whole lot of dangers out there that you just might not have considered. It is not a fun night out. Not in any sense of the word – and the paranormal has to be respected.

Before you go, take another look at that insurance policy. Make sure it's in date and will cover what you need it to. Third-party indemnity, personal accident, and maybe even your equipment too... it's all important.

Dress in suitable clothing. Make it warm and

comfortable and not something so voluminous that it could get you caught up on something.

Ensure your footwear is non-slip and durable and will protect the whole foot – no sandals or ...*horror of horrors,* flip flops.

Use a torch to move about – even if you think you can make out your surroundings well enough without, and always carry a spare. If you drop it and it breaks well, you get the idea.

When you are using your torch to move around, keep it pointed to the floor, particularly when you first turn it on. That way you'll not totally destroy your night vision, or that of your companions.

When you are out and about, keep an emergency phone with you and, of course, always let someone know exactly where you are going and what time you will be back.

Where necessary, you should notify the police or coastguard – if you are somewhere that requires it – and yes, some places do!

Most of all though, make sure you have permission to be there. Or you could risk that unforeseen danger of ending up in court.

**The Physical**

Firstly, there are the obvious physical dangers of

being out and about, maybe on your own, in a potentially ruinous building with all its associated hazards.

Before you start and whenever possible, have a good look around in natural daylight first. Taking note of all potential risks.

Look for trip hazards and signs of rotten flooring, like spongy, springy boards. Remember to look up – checking for potential overhead dangers from crumbling walls or roofs that could give way – and look out for trailing wiring or anything that you could get caught up on.

During the investigation, don't forget about the hazards that you yourself have just created. Remain aware of the exact placement of that camera tripod, beam barrier, and any other trip hazards.

Of course, lasers are a hazard in themselves, and should always be placed where no one can accidentally look into the beam.

If you are in an old derelict building, there is always a potential risk of coming into contact with asbestos. Any building built prior to 2000 could contain it – and at one stage, its use was widespread. If you're unsure about the presence of this potentially lethal substance, then always wear a suitable mask and avoid stirring it up as dust – or by breaking materials and potentially sending plumes of it airborne.

When damaged, asbestos releases tiny fibres into the

air, which if inhaled, can cause serious disease or even death in years to come.

Take no risks with it. I would simply advise that if you *know* it's there, then keep out.

Moulds are another common danger. You might think it doesn't matter – that you're not going to be in there long enough – but again, they could bring you serious respiratory problems further down the line. Protect your health while you can, and if in doubt, use an N-95 filtering respirator.

There is a greater potential danger though, and one likely to cause widespread panic in the event of a sighting. Stay safe. Stay aware of the risk, because sooner or later, you *will* be attacked by one of those eight-legged nasty's ...*Spiders!*

In all seriousness though, if there's only one bit of advice you'll take from me, let it be this. If you believe the investigation site to be in a dangerous state – for *any* reason, STAY OUT!

**The Metaphysical**

Yes, I can see you rolling your eyes now – but spiritual danger is not something to be taken lightly. I should know ...I've been there!

Firstly, and before even considering setting off, ask yourself if you are in a reasonable frame of mind – if you are in a good place emotionally for the coming investigation. You need your spiritual energy, your vibrations, to be on a high level.

Simply put, are you in a good mood?

If *not*, if you're angry, upset, or depressed then don't go.

Before starting any investigation – I would always advise everyone present to make sure they have completed, at least, a basic protection exercise. This is purely to prevent potential negative energy from getting to you – to stop it from entering.

There are countless methods for doing this, and everyone has their own. So, I will just skim over the basics of my own preferred technique.

Imagine, if you will, sending down roots from your feet, deep down into the Earth. Now visualise in your mind's eye, travelling at speed down those roots – sinking deeper and further into the Earth. Keep going – until you start to see the dazzling white light of the Earth's energy, its power. Start to draw that light back up those roots, up and into your body. Draw it into your feet – your legs – torso – arms –then finally, your head. Let it fill you completely – overflowing outwards into a bright protective bubble through which nothing harmful can pass.

Yes, it sounds weird.

But do it and mean it. It's really all about the intent, after all.

Better still though, and a much more thorough job, would be to first undergo grounding. To remove any negative energy that you may already be unwittingly carrying.

You may want to consider wearing a protective charm. Something like a pentagram, crucifix, or any other religious symbol that you have a personal faith in and many investigators do. Some, also favour the carrying of crystals or stones known for their protective qualities – like obsidian, black tourmaline, or amethyst.

Me? I always keep a pentagram with me on investigations and *no*, it's not a satanic sign – but is actually an ancient symbol of protection. Just go with what feels right for you.

Keep your wits about you.

Stay aware. Don't be taken in by a spirit mimicking a child or – worse still, a passed friend or member of your family. Check it out before you believe it – ask for proof. You may think you're dealing with a well-intentioned spirit – but bad people pretend to be good people, in order to get what they want – and so it is, too, in the spirit world.

*Please* don't ever be tempted to be like those investigators you see on tv. It is never a good idea to provoke a response or challenge a spirit. At best, you'll just look an idiot – at worst – well, you just *might* get what you asked for.

I know what you're thinking here. Ghosts can't actually hurt you, though, right?

But consider, if a spirit can move an object, then it has the potential to hurt you with it. If it can touch you, it could push you and if you happened to be on a stairway at the time... speaks for itself, eh?

Now, if that spirit were to actually possess someone, someone present in the team maybe... well, now *you're really talking!* It could potentially use them to do literally, whatever it wants.

So, what about the possibility of a demonic presence?

Personally, I'm still not sure if there is such a thing – but of course, I remain wary. After all, if there is the good, then there is also the bad.

Just as there are evil people in life, so there are in death and all too often, I have seen investigators end up with scratches, unexplained bruises and once even what seemed to be a minor burn.

Yes, I accept well enough there are evil spirits, I'm just not so sure that demons themselves are a *thing*.

And whilst we're on the subject, never let a malevolent spirit get into your head. Some will want you to be afraid. They thrive on it – and the more scared you are, the stronger they will become.

They may try to scare you into running but don't. Never do that. The potential for disaster in a dark, unfamiliar environment is huge.

Take care of each other and always have each other's back.

It is not unknown for spirit to follow you home (if you allow it – through a lack of protection), and this can majorly affect your emotional state, causing pent-up anger or depression.

If you spot the signs of any attachment in your companions, challenge them about it, and get it removed.

And then there was Ouija!

The risks of using a Ouija Board are many and varied. I don't believe them to be the *gateway to hell* that films would have you suppose, but then neither are they to be taken lightly.

The safe use of the spirit board is a complex subject that I will be covering in greater depth in a later chapter.

So – have you changed your mind yet?

Let's take it down a good few notches now and the one horror that you are most likely to come across on the average investigation, is that ultimate dread of the paranormal investigator, boredom!

• • •

At the end of the night, remember to close the investigation.

You might want to double down on your protection exercise at this point and of course, don't forget to thank the spirits for any activity, telling them to stay put and *not* to follow you home.

Investigating the paranormal is a funny old business. It can bore you to tears or, on occasion, be scary as hell. Either way always remember that in the grand scheme of things, the living, are much scarier than the dead... just not half as scary as those bloody spiders, eh?

Chapter 19
## The Attic Children
My Paranormal Experiences...

Having always lived a vaguely nomadic lifestyle *(in case you hadn't already noticed),* itchy feet had, once more, taken hold and, in 'full hunt mode', I had been enthusiastically searching for our next housing project.

I was after something different, something exciting, something we could really get our teeth into – but as yet, nothing had presented itself.

Half-heartedly now, I'd been peering over my husband's shoulder as he, once again, skimmed through the available offerings on Zoopla.

'Hey, stop a minute... go back a page.'

I looked on with growing excitement as the page reloaded.

I was right. My eyes hadn't deceived me!

There, in all its glory, was a classic brick-built early

Georgian house, in the exact search area that we had previously specified. Why hadn't this come up in *my* searches?

In my early twenties, having always held a keen interest in property, I'd begun my love affair, my deep appreciation for buildings of the Georgian era. I simply adored their style and grandeur. Their simple elegance and this one looked perfect.

Wasting no time, the very next day, I rang the agent to book an appointment, and set off with great excitement, anxious for the viewing.

So, here it was at last, *that* house. Under the watchful gaze of the town's ancient castle keep, it seemed to snuggle in – to nestle amongst the many other gorgeous examples of Georgian architecture and although decidedly smaller than that of its neighbours, it was still utterly charming.

Set over three floors, it had two fantastic sized living rooms and a workable kitchen on the ground floor, three double bedrooms on the floor above, and then – there was the third floor.

Accessed via a tiny double-twisting staircase, I breathlessly pushed open the door to reveal the strangest of spaces.

Built into the eaves, the attic room formed a sort of s-shape. An internal sash window overlooked the little stairway, letting in borrowed light from the old skylight above. Whilst at the far end, a small, many-paned dormer window offered glorious views out, through the dirt-encrusted glass, over the walled garden to the beautiful green hills beyond.

An air of light neglect pervaded the room. Old wallpaper hung everywhere – drooping like limp streamers from the steeply sloping ceilings – partially held back here and there, with sticky tape, now yellowed with age.

What a strange vibe this space held. A thick, cloying atmosphere. Not really bad – not bad at all, in fact, but somehow busy!

So, this was the reason the house hadn't shown up in my searches. I had restricted my search to four-bedroomed dwellings, but the selling agent had listed this as a three – obviously not considering this area suitable as a bedroom. It would clearly fit the bill though –at least it would, once we had ripped out the old built-in cupboards and rectified the unusual line in 'Adams Family' décor.

Yes, this was the house for us!

I did my research, of course, before the move.

A search of the Historic England website confirmed that it was a grade II-listed Georgian house. Built originally in 1764 and partially rebuilt with a new front façade after fire damage in 1931. Okay, so not perfect, but it sounded pretty damned good to me!

Life was hectic over the next few months as we worked feverishly on the restoration and that once sadly neglected attic room was soon to become the most fantastic of 'man caves' for my husband.

We'd kitted out the first part of the 'S' as a bedroom, although no one ever actually chose to sleep there. I can't say I blame them, to be honest. It was always 'spiky' up there – and left most people feeling uneasy, vaguely anxious. By then, I was fully aware that it was among the most active spots in the house.

The second part of the 'S' was a full-on man cave, complete with a stressless recliner, mini fridge, and boys' toys galore. Here my husband, oblivious to the atmosphere of the place, would happily while away his evenings.

My father happily took to the front lounge. Creating his own living room come bedroom – adoring as he did, its triple windows and view of the castle – whilst we kept the back living room for our use, with its quieter garden and countryside views. On the whole, it worked very well.

If I'm honest though, I'd known that we weren't going to be alone in that house from the moment we'd first walked in. I mean you can't buy a place *that* old, and expect there to be no ghosts now, can you?

Sometimes, there would be the *strangest* smell of smoke in the air – of sulphur mainly from the back bedroom – and enough at times to become mildly alarming. Yet as quickly as it came, it was just as soon gone again.

Visiting friends with more psychic tendencies than I *(not really difficult, in the grand scheme)* were able to help flesh out what I'd already sensed.

There was a man, they told me, a military man of rank – that liked to stand by the huge sash window of the back living room. There was a busyness about the first floor, where activity would rush between the rooms, but with a particular emphasis on the back bedroom, where they believed the fire had started.

And as for the attic room... well... let's just say that it was definitely occupied.

I always felt watched while I was in that room and couldn't go up that staircase without feeling breathless at the top.

At first, I'd reasoned that it was just because I'm old, overweight, and generally unfit – but I already knew in my heart that it really wasn't the case.

The energies within that space would somehow drain you, the moment you crossed that threshold, and it didn't just happen to me. Visitors would often remark on it, sometimes doubling over, needing to rest their hands on their knees to draw breath.

So, I knew well enough by now that our home was haunted, but the first actual sighting was to be made by my husband. Awakened in the dark of the night, he'd alarmingly spotted a small, child-sized shadow figure, flit silently across the back bedroom before exiting through the door and out into the hallway.

*Superb!*

The front bedroom too, seemed to have a dark area of its own – it drew your eye – almost as though a figure were standing there. But I never saw anything when looking directly at it, and came eventually, to simply ignore it.

Often, I would *feel* the energy of the place. I would get that buzz, that zap that meant activity was ramping up. My daughter felt it, too, on literally every occasion that she visited. At times it was like walking through a static field – and one memorable incident happened whilst she was staying with us.

She and I were chatting in the living room, the menfolk were, as ever, down the pub, and my granddaughters were both tucked up, sound asleep in the front bedroom.

For some strange reason, my daughter always preferred that the girls not sleep in the back bedroom. *Apparently*, she found the sudden, intermittent smell of burning to be disconcerting, and *(all joking aside),* that was fine by me. Quite understandable under the circumstances.

All had been calm and quiet in the house when,

without warning, energy instantly ramped up, coursing through us and treating us both to the buzz.

Stopping literally mid-sentence, we looked at each other. Quite shocked.

'Jeez, did you *feel* that?'

It was the strongest I had ever felt in that house, and it had come out of nowhere.

Alert now and on edge, we became aware of soft noises emanating from the hallway. Cautiously, we got up to investigate, quietly opening the living room door.

What a relief! There, standing halfway down the stairs, was Ashley, my beautiful second granddaughter.

'Maman… j'ai été malade. (Mummy, I've been sick). Scooping her up, we took her back upstairs to get cleaned up.

Ah, the poor little maid. She certainly *had* been sick.

I carried the still sleeping Alice (her sister) out of the room, placing her gently on my bed, while I went to help my daughter clean up Ashley.

Could that buzz have been triggered by concern for my granddaughter? Had our spirits been trying to get our attention to warn us?

I'd certainly like to think so.

I'm sure that's exactly what they'd been trying to do – and thank you!

Months passed and life settled down, and we lived

quite comfortably with our unseen companions – for the most part, anyway.

One sunny morning though, my dad didn't seem his usual self. He was quiet and withdrawn.

'What's up, you have a bad night?'

'Yes, I couldn't sleep.' He hesitated. 'I woke in the night, and someone, something, was in the room. It was standing by the fireplace. Then it walked straight past me and over to the door.'

*Wow ...impressive!*

'What did it look like?' Ever the investigator, eh?

'I couldn't tell. It was just a shadow, but in the shape of a man ...but I s*aw* it!' he added defensively, looking me in the eye, in case I should doubt him.

Why would I disbelieve him? I knew well enough by now, that we were not alone in the house.

Our lives,ours and that of our spirit house guests, coexisted happily enough, and it was here, at this house, that the incident of the missing wedding ring was actually to take place. So, it would seem that they were looking out for us.

With renovations now nearing completion, the last big task was to recarpet the attic room. No small feat this, due to its fantastically irregular shape and large size, and not to mention the tiny access stairway!

Anyway, the carpet fitter had been booked, and we had spent that day stripping out the old carpet and clearing the room as best we could. Exhausted, I went to bed early, watched a bit of tv, did a bit of internet surfing, before falling asleep happily enough. The night was still full dark, when something thumped on my ceiling, bringing me to instant wakefulness.

*What the hell...?* I glanced at the clock ...02:55!

Suddenly, there was another great thud. I stared up at the ceiling, eyes wide, as a distinctive rolling sound travelled clear across the floor up above – not unlike the sound of a large marble, the newly bared boards, making the sound loud and clear in the silence of the night.

This was nuts!

Another thud, and another, and then came the footsteps... light and fast as they skipped across the room.

What were they *doing* up there?

This was the children – it had to be...

Had they just discovered that bare boards are far more fun when it comes to making mischief? If so, they were really going for it.

I'm not going to lie – I was very uncomfortable at that point. This activity was off the scale – and was going on right over my head, in *my* house!

It'll stop in a minute, I reasoned, not wanting to have to even think about going up there. But oh no – the thuds, footsteps and some weird intermittent scraping sounds continued.

*Okay then...* maybe not.

Bracing myself, I threw back the blankets, crossed my room and pulled open my bedroom door and that, of course, is when it stopped.

Everything, *every* sound, stopped dead.

I was shocked into inaction.

Somehow, this was worse than the commotion had been. It felt *intense*, charged, as though they were aware and were waiting. Now I was really spooked.

Bravely, intrepidly, and with no thought whatsoever given to my own personal safety... I went to wake my husband, who had remained blissfully asleep throughout.

I know, I know... *I'm the investigator*!

But, in my defence, it was the early hours. In *my house*, and...

Alright! I was chicken ...I admit it.

Of course, he'd heard nothing, he saw nothing – and he was *really* pissed that I had woken him in the middle of the night and sent him upstairs for no reason.

A couple of hours later – after he'd left for work, still muttering under his breath about being rudely awakened – and something about a *'crazy bat'* that I didn't quite catch, I did manage to finally pluck up the courage to go upstairs myself.

Perplexed, my eyes swept around the near empty room. I had literally no idea what they could have been rolling. It had sounded like a marble – but there was nothing remotely like that up here, nothing that would roll anyway.

Who knows? Maybe I was going crazy, eh?

Arranging a few small items that might interest the children, I quickly set up the night vision camera and recorder – took one last, uncomfortable look around, before flicking the light off and skedaddling back down to my room – to attempt to get some sleep.

The review of that footage was to be both remarkable and disappointing, at the same time.

Although none of my trigger objects had been moved – there were sounds, taps, soft thuds and a couple of vague dragging noises.

So, I could discount the 'going crazy' idea for sure. The disappointment came, because those sounds were nothing like those that had awakened me, mere hours before.

*Then* they had been simply off the scale.

Chapter 20
# To Ouija Or Not To Ouija?
That, is the Question...

The Ouija, Talking Board ...or Spirit Board as it is often still called, has a long and strange history – and it's probably not what you'd expect.

Due to low life expectancy and high infant mortality rates, the people of the Victorian era were to become obsessed with being able to contact their departed loved ones. An idea that was then mainstream and perfectly acceptable.

Keep in mind, that this was the era of momento mori photography, the taking of post-mortem photographs of deceased family members – which were then proudly displayed on the mantelshelf to keep their memory alive.

Some of the deceased were carefully posed – attempting to create the illusion of life and, all too often, were pictured alongside their still living siblings.

Commonplace, too, in this era, was the practice of making and wearing intricate items of mourning jewellery, that would contain the plaited hair or other reliquaries of your deceased family member.

These practices were never done out of a sense of morbidity but were purely an attempt to keep a connection to those loved ones that they had so cruelly lost – it was a way of expressing their love.

During the late 1800s, a surge of interest in all things spiritual, was to result in the production and widespread use of the Ouija. Then considered a game – indeed, at the time, one of the best-selling parlour games ever.

It was marketed as 'The Magic Game' and was said to be great fun, mystifying and able to answer your questions about the past, present, and future and this *game* would be used at family gatherings for light-hearted entertainment.

It was at one point, owned and marketed by Parker Toys, who would later sell the rights to Hasbro, who still produce boards today, literally a child's toy.

So how did this innocuous beginning end up with a board that instils terror, even in today's enlightened world?

That one is easy. It's the result of a glut of movies that all featured the dire consequences of using the board. All in the name of good, healthy entertainment, of course.

...that girl, who was cruelly murdered after the board had spelt 'die'.

...the demon that can gain control of the body of the unwitting user.

The stories are many and varied – but all with the same basic theme, if you use one, you use it at your peril!

The hype and hysteria have grown exponentially over the intervening years, helped along, not a little, by the Church, who saw its surge in popularity as a potential threat to their authority. If people were led to believe it was 'the instrument of the devil' – then maybe they would steer clear and turn back to the Church for guidance.

So, what exactly *is* a Ouija?

Generally made of wood but often now available in cardboard too, a typical board will feature the letters of the alphabet from A through to Z, the numbers 0 to 9 and the words Yes, No, Hello and Goodbye.

A pointer, known as a planchette, is used to indicate the various letters and numbers, and this is achieved when all participants place a finger lightly upon it and allow it to '*do its thing.*'

Prior to this invention, people would attempt communication in precisely the same way, but did so by calling out letters of the alphabet or numbers, names etc. – and would keep going, until they got a noise of some sort in response. Obviously, a very long-winded and essentially flawed way to attempt spirit communication. I mean, what if the awaited tap were to come two seconds too late? The message is now completely ruined.

So, is it bad? Is it evil?

It's often said that using a Ouija will open the door to the spirit world – to lift the veil, if you like, but isn't that kind of the point of the thing? Surely if doors remain closed, then there can be no possibility of communication.

Have I used one?

Yes, many times and I'm still here to tell the tale.

Do I recommend you use one?

Hmmm, yes... *sort of* – but only under certain circumstances – the most important of which is, that you use it under the guidance and watchful eye of someone who knows what they are doing. It might be marketed as a toy, but it is really not.

So, are there rules for using the board?

Well, if not rules per se, then there are definitely guidelines. A list of best practices if you like. I have compiled some of the more critical pointers for you below – but I still stand by my first bit of advice, find someone that knows what they are doing – to help guide you in its use.

Before you start, first things first, decide where you are going to do this.

I would recommend avoiding its use in your home but

look for somewhere instead that is quiet and calm, where you will not be interrupted or suffer distractions.

Choose carefully with whom you are going to attempt it. There must be more than one, and not too many, which could cause sessions to become confusing and disorderly.

The need to trust your partners is paramount, and I would always advise against using the board with strangers or people you just don't know well enough. You won't know *who* they are – whether they are trustworthy – or if they'll bring bad vibes to the session.

Think about where you'll position the board. Will it be a comfortable height and reach for everyone taking part? It may seem easy at first to lean over a table – but give it ten minutes, and your arm muscles will be literally screaming.

I recommend low lighting – or if you prefer to go down the lights out route, you'll need either a glow-in-the-dark board or why not place a glowstick on the planchette.

Choose who is going to be asking the questions. It should always remain just one person throughout the whole session.

Finally, have the means to record it. Set up a camcorder or have someone film or write down the results for you.

## Opening

The norm would be to perform a short protection exercise and maybe an opening prayer. Introduce yourselves – then clear your minds and concentrate on what you want to achieve.

Everyone taking part should place a fingertip from each hand *(or one hand if space is limited)* lightly on the planchette.

The chosen guide can now ask a question. A typical question for opening a session would be something along the lines of, you guessed it... '*Is there anybody here with us tonight?*'

Be patient. It can take a long time for the planchette to respond. Don't be in too much of a rush.

## The Session

Stay with just your one allocated question asker, *the guide*. If someone else wishes to ask something, they should always direct that question through the guide.

Don't ask open questions, at least not one's that would have complicated, long-winded answers.

Never be tempted to ask a question to which you really don't want the answer, because you *might* just get it. You know what I'm getting at... don't ask anything stupid, like, 'what year will I die?' I mean... what if they were to tell you – mischievously or otherwise, that it will be soon?

Stay serious and respectful at all times

If something comes through that you *feel* to be wrong, tell them 'Thank you, Goodbye,' and close the session at once.

Watch your session partners closely, but don't be too quick to judge.

I took part in a board session once, where I became convinced that one of the team was pushing and controlling the planchette. As it turned out, I couldn't have been more wrong. As was proven a short while later when he eventually took his hands away to stretch his arms. The planchette carried on regardless, with no change in its rhythm.

**Keep Your Hands On The Planchette?**

This is a contentious issue. People have told me that you should never remove your finger until the board session is closed.

But this is not a theory that I agree with and in all honesty, I have never been able to keep my hand on the planchette for longer than five or so minutes anyway, before I get a full-on arm cramp and *have* to swap hands.

**Closing**

This is an important one. End the session. Never just stop.

Always end the session with a goodbye – and remember to thank the spirits for any response you may have had. If you started by saying an opening prayer, then at this point, I would suggest a closing prayer would be appropriate.

No matter what you do, some people will debunk your Ouija Board experience as wishful thinking – and put it down to the idiomotor response or idiomotor reflex *(different name... same thing)*.

The idiomotor reflex is a psychological phenomenon that can cause an unconscious motion. For example, if you are thinking of great Aunt Agatha – you may unconsciously bring about minute reflexive muscular actions, ones of which you aren't even aware. Still, it could be enough to help guide the planchette the *right way* and start spelling A.G.A.T... and so on.

So, is there a technique you can use to help ensure that any given communication is *real?*

Yes, for sure.

Have the guide, the person asking all the questions,

separate from the board. If they do not touch the planchette, they cannot directly influence it.

Whenever possible, ask questions to which nobody on the board will already know the answer.

Seriously, consider blindfolding the participants *(obviously – just those with their fingers on the planchette)*. Again, if they can't see, they cannot then directly influence the outcome.

I have tried this myself with some outstanding results – although most sessions, I admit, will be unsuccessful. At the very least – it will add a whole new element of eeriness to the procedure.

If you decide to go down the blindfolded route, then always film the session as a courtesy to participants. This way, they will see what actually happened, rather than just what they were *told* had happened.

Don't be afraid of the board – but be sensible.

If you get *any* sense of a problem, that all isn't well, or that something bad may have come through, then say goodbye, close the session immediately, and call it a day.

## Chapter 21
## Table Tipping
My Paranormal Experiences...

If you're looking to have a go at one of the more visually spectacular *(at times, anyway)* methods of spirit communication, then it just has to be Table Tipping.

As I have previously touched upon – participants will position themselves around a small, sturdy table – placing just their fingertips (not hands) very lightly on the surface.

Someone will take the lead and commence communication by asking any spirit present to move or rock the table.

I have witnessed a table rise onto one leg and somehow balance itself, whilst slowly swivelling around – forcing everyone taking part to quickly shuffle around in order to keep their fingertips in place.

Others have reported the table leaving the floor

completely – though I have yet to see this particular miracle occur.

The most common movement you are likely to encounter, is a steady rocking back and forth. The problem with this is that our old friend, the '*idiomotor reflex*' argument, can kick in once again.

Basically, the science says that if you all want the table to rock back and forth, then it WILL rock back and forth – but caused by a minute muscular movement that you aren't even aware of – rather than by the hand of spirit.

What you need to get past this argument – what you must aim for, is way more than just a little gentle rocking.

Ask that spirit to twist the table and turn it on the spot. Or why not ask for it to be moved across the room? And yes, I have seen this happen many times, in fact.

At one of my first investigations all those years ago at the jail – I watched, thoroughly perplexed, as the table rocked and twisted its way right out of the room, down the hallway and into another area entirely.

I couldn't believe what my eyes were telling me. I kept looking under the table, and all around – searching for anything that could be causing the movement.

I carefully studied all the hand positions of the participants, how they were standing and where they had their fee – but no, I couldn't see how any of them could be influencing the tables' bizarre dance.

Since then, I have participated in many such sessions – some of which, I can admit to being quite spectacular. The afore mentioned spinning on one leg session, was amazing to behold.

That particular table was of the four-legged variety – and somewhere in the region of three feet square.

It had rocked so much and was spending longer and longer as it balanced on each alternate pair of legs. Then, when it seemed impossible to remain balanced on just two, the third leg suddenly left the floor entirely – and it was left hovering, lightly quivering, on the one leg that remained floor bound.

I have absolutely no idea how it didn't just tip onto the floor. It seemed way past the point of no return, its balancing point – and thinking it was about to tip over, I put out a hand, towards the corner, ready to catch it before it fell – but it wasn't necessary. The table slowly twisted around on that one leg – before hovering once more.

Everyone present that night was awestruck. They looked under and around the table – careful to maintain contact with their fingers, while it just hovered there.

Then, as quickly as it had begun – it was over. It crashed back down with a thud – to rapturous shrieks of delight and much excited chatter.

Generally, as a rule, you will need at least four or five people to get a good response, but there are times when that rule has been comprehensively broken. Like the time we attended an investigation at a stately home in Devon, by the kind invitation of the owners.

With only one other team member in the mood to try table tipping that night, I shrugged and thought, why not give it a go anyway?

Taking our places opposite each other, we placed our fingertips on the tabletop – well away from the edge and started to call out. There was a slight movement, little more than a twitch, but it was a promising start.

Calling out again, we asked for the table to turn – for it to twist – and had barely got the words out when it did just that.

Grating on the stone floor, it twisted and jerked its way around, until we were literally facing in the opposite direction.

Well, to say that we were surprised would be the understatement of the year. Quite frankly, we were gobsmacked – but asking once again, for spirit to work with us and move the table – it had then proceeded to lead the two of us virtually right round that big old room.

Sometimes it took us by surprise and suddenly backtracked, as it unexpectedly twisted in the opposite direction – and all while we were watched in silent amazement by the rest of the team.

So, tell me... *how* can that be an idiomotor reflex?

I have had a table pin me to the wall once – and no,

I'm not joking. When I asked who it wanted to ask the questions – it had kept on moving towards me until my back was against the wall, literally pinning me there.

So, I guess it's me asking the next question then, eh?

I have twice had the table rocking with just me on it. But to be fair, it was only a slight rocking. Not very impressive for the beholder. VERY impressive for the only participant, though – namely me!

Impressive and awe-inspiring as some of the results of table tipping can be – there are, however, real limitations. Not on the table movement of course, that can be amazing – but there are limitations on the actual ability to communicate properly.

I mean, how do you have any kind of meaningful conversation?

You could try asking for it to turn clockwise for yes and anti-clockwise for no, of course – and yes, I have done this. But it is still an incredibly flawed method for actual communication.

From experience, sooner or later, you will run out of suitable questions with a yes or no answer – and from that point on, it's '*end of conversation*'.

It's this, 'running out of questions', and 'conversations that just peter out', through the lack of ability to take the exchange further, that is the most frustrating thing about paranormal investigating – for me, anyway.

I guess I must be greedy – because I always want more.

I want to know who the spirit is. Where they are from? – *When* they are from?

Without an appropriate means to answer such questions, though – it will inevitably end up becoming a frustrating business in the end.

## Chapter 22
# Past Lives

Yes, I mused again!

The idea that we will live more than one life in this mortal realm is not a new concept. It was a mainstay of numerous ancient cultures and features still in many religions around the world today.

Buddhism, Sikhism, Hinduism, and Paganism – amongst many others, all adhere to the principle of reincarnation – the belief that aspects of self, your very being *(your soul if you like)*, will survive death and undergo a rebirth into another bodily form.

The eventual outcome of that reincarnation will, of course, vary – depending upon the religion followed. In some faiths, you may come back as an animal, whilst others will always stick to the human form – but they are similar enough in concept, though, for me to group them together.

Furthermore, all these religions adhere closely to the notion of Karma – the doctrine that affirms that what you do in this life, you shall pay for in the next. That if you do bad things in this lifetime, you will suffer for it in the next – maybe through a severe illness, hardship, or bad luck.

These ideas are mainstream, ordinary everyday beliefs. Followers of these religions have no problem with the thought that they have lived before or that they will do so again.

So why do we westerners have such difficulty in accepting such a concept might exist?

Could it simply be that, over the centuries, our Christian religious leaders have striven to push such heathen ideas aside? To rid us of the last vestiges of paganism, the old religion of the British Isles – in the belief perhaps that it would be in conflict with the written text of the bible?

I guess it could be that. It would seem the most likely case, but now it would seem we are just too enlightened for our own good.

We have become less accepting of the old ways, more *modern* – seeing our old beliefs as archaic and somehow backward.

We used to have a reverence for nature and a deep-seated awareness of the cycle of life. We were connected with our Earth – *feeling* the changing of the seasons within us.

These days, we have moved so far from our pagan origins that we have lost all connection with the natural world around us. Just like the passing of a year, we too, are born, mature, age, and then die. But in paganism, death is but a part of life – not to be feared, but simply seen as the beginning of the next phase.

So previously, I have talked about the fact that we are an energy – and that by the First Law of Thermodynamics, energy cannot be destroyed but can only evolve and change its form.

Our energy – the energy that incorporates our personality, memories, and life experiences, *must* continue to exist, even after the death of our mortal bodies. Would it not, therefore, make sense that *our* energy – the very *essence* of who we are – would be able to reinhabit another human body as and when it had the capability and the desire to do so?

As for what purpose? Honestly? I have no idea.

Maybe it *is*, simply to learn a lesson, as some religions would have us believe. It may also be to teach us a lesson – perhaps by having to lead a more challenging life next time around. But who can really know?

There have been innumerable well documented cases of people that have claimed to remember a previous life. Many have been able to track down proof of their past existence. They've been able to give full details... names, dates, places – minutiae of their prior self, of someone they couldn't possibly have known existed by any other means.

Usually, it is as young children that these past memories come to the fore – before the child has had a chance to 'grow out of the memory' or be convinced by their current family that it's simply their vivid imagination playing tricks upon them.

However, *if* the family is prepared to take the child's claims seriously, as I am convinced, they should, then it might be possible to find that evidence – as has been accomplished in the past.

One such example is the case of James – a reincarnated airman, killed during the second world war. His family listened to what he had to say and managed to find proof of his previous life. They located the records of the ship on which he was stationed. Found his name in the muster roll, and even the specifics of how and where he died. All details that the 'new' James *(yes, he was even given the same birth name)* had remembered.

I am not a follower of any particular religion – I just do my own thing and live life in a simple, respectful way. I treat others well and hope to receive similar in return, but I accept that it won't always happen that way.

So, do I believe that we live more than one life?

Well, I think that we can, yes – if we *choose* to. Although I have to wonder sometimes, what the attraction would be. I mean, it's hardly a thrill ride down here now, is it?

My thoughts aren't based on any one idea. They're not from a book I read, or some programme on tv, but they have just evolved – slowly – over the years.

Yes, I have come to believe that reincarnation can happen and that past lives can be real, and I will attempt now to explain what has brought me to this point – to run through some things that I feel may help validate my belief.

First and foremost, and you must remember here that you are talking to a paranormal investigator, is ghosts.

Yes, you read that right! I genuinely believe that the existence of ghosts can be explained within the theory of reincarnation.

If you accept, as I do, that when the body dies, our 'essence' will revert back to energy, then let's follow that path to its logical conclusion. *(Well... logical to me, anyway.)*

Just suppose, for reasons unknown, that this *essence* is not yet ready to move on – neither back into the ether nor into a new body. Could this, halfway house perhaps explain the presence of ghosts in our world?

While they are *waiting* – or perhaps even temporarily trapped – could this energy somehow show itself in the form of paranormal activity?

I believe that it does. That same ethereal energy

could interact, causing changes to our material surroundings that would appear, to our eyes, as paranormal phenomena – a haunting.

It could also explain why spirits don't seem to stay beyond a few hundred years at most. I mean, no one ever reports seeing a caveman ghost, do they? We get spirit cats and phantom dogs often enough – so where are all the ghostly dinosaurs? My theory is that it's because they have all, long ago, moved on – into their next incarnation.

The next piece of evidence I would like to lay before you – to make my case that reincarnation may really occur, is déjà vu. Literally translated from the French as 'already seen' – déjà vu is having the firm belief or feeling that you are in a place or situation that has happened to you before.

Have you ever been travelling, say to a new part of the country – somewhere you have never been – yet have rounded a corner and somehow just known precisely what you were going to see? You already know the place – the houses, the layout of the streets, even that bridge over the stream, with the old letter box embedded in it. It's like you have been there before – maybe in another life.

Equally, it could be a snatch of conversation, a weird feeling of synchronicity that you have done or said that exact same thing before.

Some people will take this to be evidence of a past

life memory. But equally, it could just be that a similar corner, in another village, had triggered a long-forgotten memory – and that memory had somehow overpainted the 'new.' Maybe that snatch of conversation had actually happened before – or at least, something near enough to trigger the response – but you had simply forgotten about it.

Do I think déjà vu can be taken as a sign of a previous life? Yes, for sure – but you will need far more specific proof than just unaccountably seeming to recognise somewhere.

For it to be taken seriously, you must come up with verifiable data – names, dates, addresses... things that can be physically checked. Then surely it can be of real interest.

Closely related to déjà vu, is the strange phenomenon of seemingly having other people's memories. Remembering conversations with people you have never met or having intimate knowledge of a house you don't know and never owned.

Evidence of reincarnation could present itself in people, as extraordinary knowledge, or skills. There are some people in history, that have seemed centuries ahead of their time. Leonardo da Vinci – painter, sculptor and inventor of machines that wouldn't appear in real life for hundreds of years. Nikola Tesla, whose work on alternating current would give rise to our modern world.

Where did these people get their ideas from – their genius? Could it be that they were, perhaps, 'old souls?'

Could recurring dreams maybe be taken as a sign of having lived before? You know the sort of thing... constantly dreaming about an accident – an event that has never happened to you. Or maybe walking through a wood, to a building that you somehow know, yet have never actually been to. Could they be some sort of throwback? A memory from a previous existence?

Irrational fears or phobias could, perhaps, be caused by traumatic experiences that have happened to us in our past lives. If, in a previous life, you had died in a mine shaft, for example – would it not stand to reason that it could cause a fear of enclosed dark spaces? A fear that would have no place in your current life – but would impact upon it, nonetheless.

Finally, what about the concept of soul mates? That special soul. That energy that you reconnect with life after life?

Yes, I know it sounds twee, but what if it's true? What if that person you've only just met, yet already feel intimately connected with, were a 'soul' that you have met before – possibly many times?

I mean, it's feasible, isn't it? Particularly if you consider the option that we may have *chosen*, where and when we came back into this mortal world.

So, there you go, my reasons for coming to believe that reincarnation may be a plausible concept.

Now I know what you're going to say here…

That same law, 'The First Law of Thermodynamics,' – also stated that the amount of energy and matter contained within the Universe, remains a constant. So, what about population growth?

What? - You weren't going to say that?

The population of the Earth has grown exponentially over recent centuries, hasn't it? So, if people are energy and energy cannot be created – where have all the extra people come from?

Well, I really don't know.

But isn't it at least possible, that it's just simply much more popular these days, to pop down to Earth for a bit of '*human time*', than it ever was in the past? …Like it's suddenly the '*in place*' to go!


So, supposing that you now consider reincarnation to be a viable prospect – have *you* ever thought about trying to find out if you have lived a past life?

Believe it or not, it just might be possible. Regression, the revisiting of past lives, may be achievable whilst under hypnosis.

Many hypnotists out there claim to be able to perform

this service. As ever, though, I strongly advise you to check their credentials and ask for reviews.

Think long and hard, to make sure that it is something that you definitely want to do. Don't forget that we're talking about your past *lives* here... so obviously, you will have gone through periods of stress, pain, and death. Is this something you really want to be reminded of?

If you decide to go ahead, you should take a friend with you, for support, in case things get emotional – and make sure that the session is recorded so you can review it properly, in your own time.

Who knows, you may have another lifetime's worth of experiences to open up – to get to know who you *really* are.

Chapter 23
# Paranormal Experiments
Having Fun with Spirit...

Spirits don't like to be tested. Try asking them to find the penny under the cup, a simple one in three chance, and they will get it wrong every time. That in itself is weird. I mean, surely, they should get it right at least one time out of every three – if only to be in line with luck alone?

No – I believe they do it on purpose, to prove a point. '*Do not test us.*'

You have to accept their existence – to believe.

That said – if you have accepted and you *do* believe – then the spirit world is not above having a bit of fun – and on occasion, we have taken full advantage of this with great success.

Like the time that just two of us were given the run of a renowned haunted castle. The whole place to ourselves. What an opportunity!

It's amazing what a difference it can make, to have a place like that to yourself. The atmosphere is just so different. Somehow more *intense*.

Anyway, the night was turning out to be good one and activity was ramping up. The Mel Rem had already lit up several times, and seemingly in answer to our many questions.

Still keen to push things just that little bit further though, I had asked spirit if they could light the device to red – requiring the strongest level of interference within its generated electromagnetic field.

Which... it promptly did!

Okay, I thought – let's see what else you can do.

'Thank you. That's fantastic. But I wonder... can you make the blue bulb light up this time? Can you turn the device blue?'

I really wasn't expecting anything much here.

To activate the blue bulb, the required amount of interference within its generated field, is two levels below that of the red – fourth in a row of six coloured LEDs – indicating the six levels of intensifying interaction.

To light it, you would need to hold your hand a precise distance from the device's antenna – and to hold it steady at that point. Pretty specific and definitely a hard ask.

But light it, they did!

The device sounded, and the blue bulb flashed into life.

Ever one to push my luck though, I just had to do it one more time. I immediately requested that they light the green bulb.

Well – I think my expression would have said it all that night. The look of shocked amazement on my face as that green bulb promptly lit, would have been evident to all. Don't you just love it when things work out!

So, here's an odd question for you...

Have you ever thought about playing cards with a ghost?

I have! And let me tell you, when it comes to games of chance, spirit definitely has the advantage over us.

With a shuffled pack of cards lying face down on the table in front of us, we set up the voice recorder – and laying a hand on the top card in readiness to turn it, I pressed record.

'What card is this? Do you know?'

We waited ten seconds before stopping the recording and immediately playing it back.

Just one little word. '*Eight*', was the EVP reply.

And sure enough, when we turned over the card, there was the eight of clubs. In stunned silence, we looked at each other. Could it really be?

'...and this one?'

We'd had one perfect response but could it be done

again? We made to repeat the experiment with the next card and on playing back the recording – there was the soft, childlike voice once again – and this time it was unmistakable.

'*It's a three.*'

Turning over the card – Oh my God-*YES!* It was the three of diamonds.

Wow – just wow! How awesome was *that*!

Not only had they picked the right number for both those cards, AND managed to convey the answer to us via the voice recorder – but they had done it, whilst the cards were still face down!

Now I have to disclose here, that this was the end of that particularly remarkable run of communication.

Sadly, nothing of note followed – but I say again… WOW!


So, how about playing long-distance guess the object with spirit? And when I say long distance – I'm really not kidding.

So, what does this involve? I hear you cry.

Well – it involves setting up a YouTube link, a live-streamed event with many people watching at the time. The potential to make complete arses of ourselves was *huge* – and I would hazard a guess that a good few of those watching that night, would've been hoping for just such an event. A bit of light entertainment, eh?

So, me in my house, my teammate in hers and some twenty miles between us. At her place, she had the spirit box running – whilst at mine, I had previously selected several objects at random. I was holding one now, in my hand – being careful to keep it shielded and well away from the camera link, so that she couldn't see what it was.

The object of the exercise? To request that any spirit present with her should jump over to me – take a look at what I was holding and then return – and using the spirit box for communication, let her know what it was.

Well, believe it or not, it wasn't that long before she heard the word '*key*', and I ended that session by displaying the house key that I had been holding, to the camera.

Again, we tried it.

This time I had a button. That was an easy one – the answer came almost instantly and then it was a feather...

Each time, my teammate was able to pluck those words from the sounds that the spirit box was making – even though she had no prior clue as to what I'd chosen.

But hang on a minute... what if we'd been cheating? What if we had prearranged the items?

Well, I can only assure you that we certainly had not.

Upping the stakes big time now, and without any prior

thought or discussion beforehand – I asked if anyone currently watching wanted to take part.

A lady from Canada messaged to say that she would love to try. So, I requested that she find an object, anything she liked, and to hold it in front of her, concentrating on it.

My co-player then asked the seemingly impossible, for spirit to travel over to Canada – find this random woman – have a good look – and report back to us what this new and unexpected participant was holding.

Well, as you can imagine, I was actually anticipating that this attempt would fail and fail big style.

We listened so hard to the sounds of that spirit box. Tentatively, we tried a few possible words but then clearly heard '*sewing box*'.

'That's it!'

The words typed swiftly across the screen. The excitement from across the pond was evident. '...I had my sewing box on my knee!'

Ah, those spirits! They are clever little so and so's at times, eh?

One of the more exciting experiments to do on an investigation, is to ask spirit to do something to someone in another room. The intended target wouldn't have known anything about your request, but you often get to *hear* if it has been acted upon.

There's nothing more satisfying than asking spirit to touch someone in another room, and then hearing their surprised shriek a few seconds later.

Ah, the joy.

If you want to make your contact with spirit more diverting, then why not give them something fun to interact with? The use of trigger objects can raise interest in the spirit world. Like the use of EMF Bears or indeed, any small toy – should you believe child spirits to be present.

Arrange the objects and either set up a locked-off video camera, take still photos to accurately show the position of all items, or maybe even draw around them to highlight any possible movement. Then invite spirit to come and have fun.

If you get it right and have articles that they can relate to – you just might get that desired interaction.

Sometimes though, it is us that are put to the test.

When undergoing a Ouija board session in a local pub at the landlord's request – we later found out that he had pre-written some words on a piece of paper that he'd sealed in an envelope. Words, he believed, were relevant to the questions that he wanted us to ask spirit.

I think he got quite a shock that day, when three of

the four words and phrases were to come out during that session.

Of more interest to me though was the near-full pint glass that was somehow scat from the table in another totally empty section of the room and during that same session.

Happy days...

## Chapter 24
# The Typical Investigation

To give you an inkling of what can happen during a typical paranormal investigation, I have included a couple of report excerpts from years gone by. These are not written to thrill but are simply a record of what was experienced on the night and I have included them only so you'll know what sort of *excitement* you can expect.

Most investigations *(if I'm honest),* verge on the boring. So please don't go nodding off on me.

**A Little Cornish Castle**

The night of the investigation was cold but clear, with a light south-westerly breeze.

We were excited for the night ahead and eagerly anticipating the coming investigation, due to the plethora of previously reported paranormal activity at this historic location.

On arrival, we completed a walk-through of all available rooms – checking for power sources, WIFI points or anything else that could cause our equipment to malfunction. Baseline checks were completed, and any points of interest, duly noted.

The castle is laid out over four floors and is basically just one room on each level (with the exception of the ground and first floors, which have additional doorways leading to private accommodation), with just a single stone spiral staircase connecting the levels.

We had previously decided to start on the upper levels and to work our way down as the night proceeded. After completing standard grounding and protection exercises, we began by spacing ourselves out around the upper floor bedroom – and commenced the investigation by introducing ourselves.

We asked a series of questions but got no audible response – except what was agreed by all, to be more of a vibration than a noise. It was almost as though someone had taken a step within the room.

A light shuffle-type noise was heard outside the door at this point, from the granite stairway and we were all quite certain that someone must have been there – but on checking, there was nothing visibly present.

We continued to ask questions and call for answers.

Looking through the monitor of the night vision camera, a light anomaly was seen floating down from the ceiling – it hovered slowly about the bed, before slowly fading out. Seconds later, it reappeared to the right, circled one of the posts of the four-poster bed before shooting downwards and disappearing once again.

This same tiny ball of light, unseen with the naked eye, appeared several more times throughout our vigil in this room. Later examination of the film was unable to debunk it as being an insect or particle of dust. There were simply no tell-tale characteristics present, wing pattern, movement etc.

Other notable events to happen during this filming session were that the camera, securely fixed on a sturdy tripod, suddenly panned to the left, for no known reason – and on several occasions, a peculiar musty smell would appear. Quite potent, only to be instantly gone again as soon as it was remarked upon.

Two of the team attempted glass divination – but although there was a slight movement of the glass, nothing of note occurred except, I should add, the reappearance of the light anomaly. This time it came from the bed and swooped down over the glass.

It was time to move on, so we gathered our kit and made our way to the room below, to set up for the next vigil.

This room is used as living accommodation and

furnished with imposing antique furniture and many interesting historic items. In the centre is a large table, and we each took a seat around it.

The atmosphere in this room felt entirely different to that above. It seemed, somehow, oppressive – darker.

An old grandfather clock with a very loud tick, stood in one corner, and one of the team asked if any spirit present could stop the clock. As if to order, the ticking slowed and seemed to hesitate, before recommencing as before. This happened a few times, seemingly on command – but regretfully we were not filming at the time so were unable to get later verification.

The last vigil of the night was in the second-floor display and meeting room. Again, we spaced ourselves around the room, and I grabbed the chair next to a small alcove.

As I sat, I became somehow *detached* from the others. I was vaguely aware that someone was talking to me, asking if I was okay, yet I felt unable *(or unwilling)* to answer. Concerned, they insisted that I move, and another team member took my place instead.

I was now 'back in the room' and entirely focused on what we were doing, but it was now the turn of my substitute to become distant and unresponsive. It was almost like turning on a switch – it was that quick.

The only other thing of particular interest that night, was that one of the solid and hefty doors, which had been left wide open when we went for a break, was found to be virtually closed upon our return.

There was no through breeze, and no one could have gotten up there, as they would have had to pass us along the way.

All in all, it was a great night of investigating with some interesting activity recorded throughout.

**A Night Out At The Cinema**

The night of the investigation was fine and warm – with no wind.

We were attending this unusual venue at the kind invitation of another team. Once we got underway, however, we split down into our respected groups, spacing ourselves well apart in the building to avoid possible noise contamination.

Our first vigil was to be in screen 2. At one time, screens 1 and 2 were one enormous room and would have formed the original theatre.

We spread out around the room, staying quiet for a while in order to get acquainted with the base sounds of the building, although it soon became apparent that there were already noises in the room that didn't originate from us.

We were all motionless, yet there were the sound of light footsteps, and on several occasions, what seemed to be the creaking of theatre chairs - as though someone were shifting their weight.

The source of these noises remained a mystery however, as wherever we placed ourselves in the room, they seemed always to come from the other side.

At one point – three of the five people present saw a shadow moving along the lefthand wall – as though someone were heading up towards the exit. All the team were stationary at the time, and there were no windows or outside sources of light that could have accounted for it.

Our second vigil of the night was to be Screen 3. However, this area proved uneventful – *it felt flat*. After a short while here, we shifted ourselves into the ladies' toilets – where there had been reports of visitors seeing apparitions and people had even been scared out of the room.

Although we were there for quite some time, the scariest thing to happen was when the automatic air freshener unexpectedly went off – you should have seen them move!

After a brief break, during which I took the only photo to show anything out of the ordinary (a vague white mist, on the upper landing) – we headed for Screen 1 and our last vigil of the night.

Here, I decided for the first time ever to attempt automatic writing, and sitting in the pitch-black auditorium, I loosely held a pen onto a sheet of plain paper, relaxed and waited.

It took quite a while, but the pen started to jerk slightly in my hand – and then to move slowly but firmly across the page.... an extraordinary sensation and quite unnerving to begin with.

When it got to where I judged the edge of the sheet to be, I turned on my torch – but was disappointed to see that it was only a jagged line. I tried again. This time, it was much more like writing, with loops and swirls – but I still couldn't make anything out.

At this point, another investigator had come into the room. She was excited to see what was going on, and I offered her the pen so that she could have a try herself.

Although she too, had never done this before, the pen moved yet again – and this time it went across the sheet in a rush.

What we got when we turned the light on amazed us all. In the middle of the swirls and loops, it read '*me - help me - agnes - hello*'.

Deeply disturbed by those words and reluctant now to

continue, we had to convince her to carry on. I'm so glad she did, though.

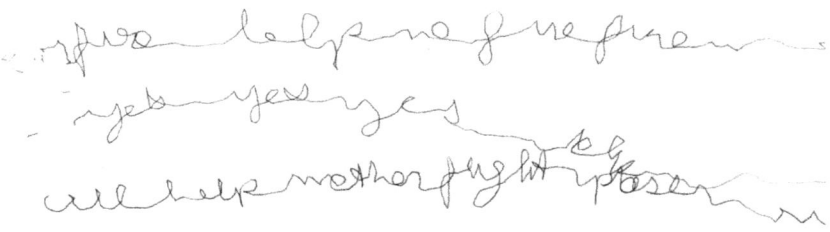

The second attempt read, *'fire - help me - fire - fire'*. This was phenomenal, and beyond my wildest expectations.

Immediately we called out to Agnes, 'Was there a fire? – and back came the next line *'yes - yes - yes,'* followed by something unreadable, then 'help (me?) – flight' and again, something we couldn't make out.

The last readable line was the most disturbing. It seemed to say ' – needs me - help agnes breathe.'

We were all understandably shocked and visibly moved by these events – and even more so when we all heard what sounded like a quiet female sigh, from an empty corner of the room – just as the last message came through and the Trifield Meter had simultaneously registered an inexplicable peak of EMF.

The last thing we wanted to do right then was leave – with so much activity going on – but it was chucking out time now, and we simply had no choice.

As it happened though, the most amazing bit of evidence of all *(to me anyway)* came the next day as I sat studying the results of the automatic writing session.

I thought I'd take another look at my efforts – and what I saw truly shocked me to the core. There, in the middle of the first line (what I had assumed to be just a scribble) was the word '*agnes*'. And more... in my second attempt, only identifiable due to my growing familiarity with her later efforts, were the words, '*help me*' and '*fire.*'

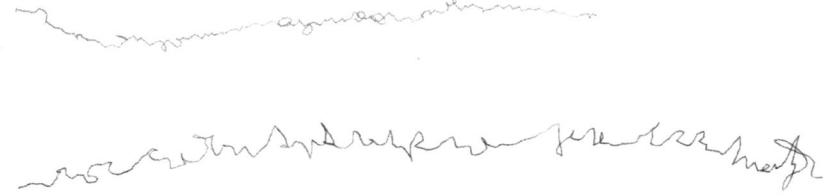

This is the proof that I had been looking for.

How could it be possible to have come up with the exact same four words? '*Agnes, help me, and fire*', when it had been a different person holding the pen – and she hadn't even been present in the room for my attempts?

She hadn't seen them –hell – *I hadn't even seen them myself!*

We would have loved to have traced Agnes' existence, but to this day, have been unable to find any information about a fire at the theatre – or about any event to happen there in which anyone was hurt.

However, it could possibly have occurred during the war, as the city had been extensively bombed.

This is what it's all about for me.

I am very fortunate to have been able to investigate some of the most incredible places in Cornwall and around the country – but a connection like this is something that I will always look back on with fond memories.

It is truly an honour to me.


Before I leave this subject altogether and move on however, I have a postscript here that I need to add.

That automatic writing session was literally the first time that either of us had ever attempted that particular method of communication.

It was an unforgettable experience and one that had taken us all by surprise.

I have made numerous attempts since then, to make contact via this technique, ALL without any significant success.

Yes, I've had lines drawn, and plenty of scribbles – but not once have I even come close to getting a word, let alone the spectacular results of that first attempt.

I can only assume that it was simply a case of being in the right place, at the right time.

*Agnes had been waiting.*

## Chapter 25
# The Ouija Board & Alice
My Paranormal Experiences...

You've met my mum before, haven't you? That lovely lady with the gorgeous smile – used a butterfly to send me a message? YES... you got it!

It's been a long fifteen years now since she departed this world for better things – and miss her as I do, I have never felt totally alone.

I still get a *feeling* – a sense of her presence from time to time – and that just has to be enough.

Well, it's not as if I've any real choice in the matter, is it?

So about five years ago, as a team, we went through a more evidence-based phase – with investigations conducted under more controlled conditions rather than whilst out and about here, there, and everywhere.

We spent considerable time in our base room, with locked-off cameras –attempting various methods of communication over and over.

This particular evening however, it was the turn of the Ouija board – or to be precise, our Ouija table.

I had converted a three foot round table into a functioning Ouija by adding the various numbers, letters, and words. It worked a treat and was large enough that the picking out of individual letters was a breeze.

We had already successfully used it on numerous other occasions, so I had high hopes for the evening – although of course, nothing in the paranormal can ever be assured.

As ever, we started the session by doing our personal protection techniques, introducing ourselves and announcing our intention to communicate through respect.

That evening was hard going. Communication was no great shakes and although we'd had snatches of activity, it was nothing to write home about.

We'd been trying now for close to two hours and were almost at the point where we were willing to call it a day – and that is when things started to change. The atmosphere within the room grew somehow prickly, spiky

– and I just knew I was in the presence of something important.

'Is there a spirit with us now?' That standard 'go to' question.

The planchette moved smoothly right around the table, in a great sweeping arc before stopping firmly on the word 'yes'.

'Do we know you?' – again, once around the table and back to 'yes'.

'Are you connected to someone in this room?'

I had known it would happen even before it had started to move. The planchette came smoothly and unhesitatingly, straight towards me.

'Is that you, mum?' but I really didn't need to ask. I could sense her presence – the warmth of her love for me.

Round the table the planchette flew, past the yes, past everything.

Twice more it circled, in large sweeping movements, before hesitating and crossing the table. Heading for the numbers 8 – 9, it slowed but didn't stop. It passed 0 and then settled on 'A'.

'Okay, thank you – A.' The planchette immediately started moving again, tracing its way along the letters, to settle once more on 'L'. Okay, so she was writing my name...

Moving on... I expected the planchette to double back, to return to the L, but it didn't. It kept going – 'I'.

'A - L - I, thank you, keep going.'

It was the following letter though, that made her intentions perfectly clear. The planchette settled on the letter 'C'.

'ALICE! - you're talking about Alice.'

I was ecstatic. My granddaughter Alice, then barely five years old, had been born six whole years after my mother passed. She had never met her – and yet here she was, talking about her!

'Are you trying to tell me that you've seen Alice?' Well, that planchette literally flew across that table, straight to the word 'yes'!

Persevering even in my overawed state, I anxiously awaited the next revelation. Round the table went the planchette, but it was slowing – getting harder now. It crawled on the 'L'.

'Okay, 'L' Thank you, what's next?'

Slowly – oh so very slowly – it crawled past M - N - O and stopped.

That was it! The end of our communication. My dear mum had run out of steam. But I knew now that she was aware of, and had been visiting Alice and I'm pretty damned confident that the last word she had been attempting to spell, had been 'LOVE'.

The energy in the room had died, it felt flat once

more – but for me, it was such a wonderful experience. I was overjoyed.

That night, as soon as I got home, I rang my daughter to explain what had happened. Well, as you can imagine, there were lots of tears and more than a little laughter too. But between us, we formulated a plan. We intended to seek confirmation, one way or another.

My daughter managed to find a rare photo of my mum, tucked away in the writing desk. My mother had always had a real phobia of cameras, and it's partly why I feel so bereft now. The images of her are too few and far between.

Anyway, she was able to find one eventually – and at the same time had also picked out two other photos of random people.

The next day, she took her chance – while Alice was sitting on the floor crossed-legged in front of the telly.

Picking out one of the random pictures, she held it out.

'Alice, have you ever seen this lady?'

Alice briefly looked at the photo, before shaking her head and turning back once more to her viewing.

Taking out the next picture. My daughter again raised it for inspection.

'What about this one Alice? Do you know this person?'

Frowning now, Alice sighed heavily as she was called

once more from her viewing. But dutifully taking a look, she again shook her head. 'No.'

So, this was it – this one would tell.

Taking the photo of my mum – an image that the kids had never seen, *could* never have seen, – my daughter held it out.

'Alice, do you know *this* person?'

More than a little irritable now at the continued interruptions, my granddaughter turned once more, to look. Suddenly, all signs of annoyance drained from her face – and were replaced now with a beaming smile.

'Yes …of course!'

This was incredible. Alice had answered as though it was the silliest question ever.

'Where do you see this person?'

'In my room – and sometimes at school.'

As you would expect, my daughter was getting pretty emotional now – and was fighting back the tears. This was more than we could have dreamed of.

'Alice, do you know who this person is?'

She shook her head vehemently. 'No' – but then she smiled, adding, 'But I like her. She's a nice lady.' – And with that, she turned her attention firmly back to the cartoon.

. . .

That was without a doubt, the most crucial piece of paranormal evidence I have ever come across. Oh, not for the others of course, though it was of interest to them too. But for me – my daughter – and although she didn't know it – for Alice.

My mother had clearly been visiting for years, and Alice being so used to it, had simply taken it as an everyday occurrence. Just another visitor – but obviously a very nice one.

That day, I thought long and hard about whether or not I should tell my father. I didn't want to risk upsetting him. But in the end, I simply decided that he had the right to know. She was his wife, and they had known each other literally their whole lives.

It was a difficult conversation – and after I'd finished recounting what had happened, there were tears in his eyes as he reached for my hand.

But I had done right after all. They were happy tears.


As I write this and stir all those beautiful memories, I am reminded that many years have now gone by since that distant day.

My daughter and I have recently revisited the subject and discussed what happened and how it had affected us.

My dear little Alice is now, *a not so little*, nine years

old – and although she remembers the photo and is fully aware that it's of her great-grandmother, she now has no recollection of ever meeting 'the nice lady.'

It's just one photo amongst many others – of people she's never met and doesn't know.

I find that incredibly sad, but I am not in the least surprised and it can only be that one of two things has happened.

Either my mum has stopped visiting – perhaps she has moved on, gone on to the next stage in her existence, maybe? – Which *is* a possibility, as I haven't had a sign from her for many months now.

Or – and I tend to believe this is the likelier of the two – Alice has simply outgrown her ability to connect with the spirit world.

After all, isn't that the normal order of things?

Chapter 26

# Our Natural State Of Being

Yes, I Have Thought Some More...

This could come across as more than a little weird to you *(Ha ha... as if you didn't already think I'm weird! eh?)*, but I have come to the conclusion that this life –this *existence* of ours, is probably not the real deal.

Oh, it seems real enough. We hurt when we fall – we bleed when we are cut – and we struggle to achieve a better, more fulfilled life – but is all this 'real'?

What is she talking about now? I hear you cry.

What do I *even mean* by that?

Let's backtrack for a moment, if I may, and go back once more to my thoughts on energy.

I have shared with you that it's my belief that life, death and pretty much everything in between, is all about energy. That energy drives literally everything, and that by the First Law of Thermodynamics, energy cannot be destroyed, but only evolve and change its form. *(I know, I know... sorry... that again!)*

So, the body has died. The energy, that was the very essence of that person, has now left and gone into the ether.

*What if*, our existence is not what we think it is?

*What if*, our life as we live it now, is NOT the main event?

*What if* our true selves, our natural selves, is actually our energy form, and that when our body dies on Earth, it's not an ending, but actually a birth, a rebirth – back into the form that we originated from? A return home, back to the place *(dimension maybe)* that we've originally come from.

Is that so crazy?

I really don't know – maybe it is – but it is where my thoughts lead me. I'm sharing them with you, not to convince you to change your beliefs. I would never do that. I'd never WANT to do that. I share them solely to start you thinking more about the strange world around us.

Let's just play the game for a moment. Just suppose that I was right. What would that mean for this life – this existence? What would it all have been *for*?

Well, that's the trick, isn't it? And who can know?

Could it be some kind of test? A learning session, maybe? Or some sort of hyper-reality holiday? The possibilities are many, for sure.

Let's take a look a look at possible supporting evidence for my theory though.

Obviously, number one, has to be the existence of the paranormal. I am just going to take a liberty here and assume that by now, you think there's a reasonable chance that the paranormal does indeed exist.

So, if we accept that the paranormal exists, then could it be that beings in their natural energy state are interfering – somehow influencing the players in the game... yes, I mean *us*!

And the game is?

Well – it's whatever this existence, is actually all about.

Another aspect of our everyday lives that could maybe support my theory is dreams. Those weird and wonderful occasions where you find you can fly, or morph through scenes of your life – to be in one place one minute, then another, within the blink of an eye.

Could they possibly be more like a memory? Of you, but while you were in another form, where the rules of this world, gravity, space, and time, just don't count.

Next on the list of possible supporting evidence will be meditation. During this process, we can often access the spiritual world around us. We can seemingly receive information, and messages from outside our earthly existence. Are we just using a form of communication that would have been natural to us, were we still in our energy form?

I believe that it's possible.

So, what of people that possess healing powers? Could they maybe be using a latent skill, a remnant of what their abilities would have been whilst in their natural form?

Many people claim to be able to heal without even the necessity of touch. It's more commonplace than you would think. Think Reiki…

Reiki is a complementary therapy that strives to clear any stagnant or blocked energy within your body – enabling your energy to flow freely once more around your body. Thus, creating balance and healing.

Both physical and mental trauma can cause stagnant energy.

Practitioners can release any blockages and guide your energy to flow correctly. They do this by the transfer of their own energy – or by pulling back some of yours, into themselves – and they do this either by the lightest of touches or, more usually, by holding their hands just above your body.

Improved energy flow around your body should relieve pain and aid relaxation.

During sessions, some people will feel instantly relaxed, whilst others may feel totally drained. On occasion, though, people can feel nauseous during or after the session. This is a physical reaction to the release of previously blocked energy and is nothing to be concerned about.

What if this type of spiritual transfer of energy was something commonplace in our other existence? Maybe whilst we were in that form, even more extraordinary feats could be done.

Finally, on my list, there is love. Love is an energy that transcends time itself. When we truly love, the passage of time and the effects of distance are as nothing. If you have ever truly loved and been loved, that feeling – that power, remains with you always. You have a genuine connection.

True love is not the selfish kind that demands physical presence all the time. It's love that you can sense around you. You can *feel* the love between you, even though you may be separated.

All transcending love of this nature is a true gift, a remnant, I believe, from our energy form existence – where connections of this sort are more the norm.


Okay, so I have shared my thoughts – I have taken up your time and dragged you down the rabbit hole, that is my very peculiar mind – and now I will make you this promise...

'I do solemnly swear, not to come up with any more totally bizarre and crackpot theories!'

There, how's that?


*By the way...* does it count if I had my fingers crossed?

Chapter 27
# A Sense Of Place
What Makes a Place Haunted?...

What exactly is it that makes a place '*haunted*'?

Is it considered so, only if there are repeated documented accounts of a ghostly sighting? Or could it be that all that is really required, is for the place to evoke feelings of vague unsubstantiated unease in the unsuspecting visitor?

If the latter is the case, which I lean towards being the more likely of the two, then, of course, there are many such places. Remember those 'dark parts' of the moor that I was telling you about? A prime example!

Some categories of building seem naturally prone to being 'haunted'. Many are places that are, and were full of life – the very heart of the community. Important to people in life and therefore important to spirit *after* life, maybe? The obvious case in point, being the public house – our beloved British pub and in particular, the coaching inn.

It's uncanny how many of these buildings are said to hold spirits – to be haunted. Surely there can be very few pubs that can't claim a spirit or three, and I'm not talking about the alcoholic variety here! Moreover, it would perhaps be easier in this case, to actually catalogue pubs that *weren't* believed to now be tenanted by ghosts.

So, the clientele of generations past had loved spending time at their favourite inn – that's a given. But would that also make it likely they'd choose to pass a considerable portion of their afterlife there too? You'd think not – yet the many reports of hauntings speak for themselves, don't they?

For me, I think there has to be something more to it, something drawing spirit back and I start to wonder… could it be that energy, that very life force that still resides within the place? It's bustle – it's hectic, *full of life* atmosphere. Could that perhaps, be what lures these spirits back?

Maybe they crave that sense of camaraderie, the vitality. It's certainly an idea. I mean, think about it – if you were able to choose where to haunt, would you prefer that quiet, sombre dwelling or somewhere full of life – with something always going on? I know what my choice would be.

In the world of paranormal investigation, it's well

known that you always get the most activity when there is plenty going on.

You could sit for hours at a time, quietly calling questions, staying silent and still in between, patiently waiting for some sign or response. But nothing happens. It's not till you give up. Stand up, stretch, and start gathering the gear while chatting and laughing, that you'll suddenly get the door swing open on its own.

And that's how it goes. Spirit will come to you when you are least expecting it. Not when you are scared, nervous or spooked *(at least, not usually)*. No, they'll come while you are laughing and joking, while you are singing to yourself at the top of your voice in that god-awful warble that makes everyone wince. I mean, if you were in their position, wouldn't you do the same?

Furthermore, as I follow my train of thought – it occurs to me that these 'spirits' themselves, are also 'of a type.' They are invariably good-natured, often mischievous, and prone to playing pranks.

In my local, the renowned and very haunted Jamaica Inn, beer glasses are regularly thrown from the shelves, and near-full pints of beer placed on the table have been known to shatter inexplicably. Is it malicious? No… never. I regard it as nothing more than pure high spirits, *(no pun intended)* …a stunt – a chance to make people sit up and pay attention.

So, what of the spirits that dwell in other locations, that are also renowned for being haunted?

Those poor spirits, for example, that are forever attached to buildings with a darker past. You know the sort of places I'm talking about – workhouses, prisons, old psychiatric hospitals, and mental asylums.

Are the spirits that reside in these places still drawn to its life force? Well, no. I would have to assume not.

Drawn, they are, but not drawn in quite the same way. It's as though these poor souls are trapped, that they are prevented somehow from leaving in the first place. Again, I would suggest that *these* spirits also seem to be of a type. Not mischievous or attention seeking, but angry, vengeful, frightened, and watchful. These are not places that anyone would choose to spend their eternity. So what keeps them there? What could the various spirits from these institutions of the past all have in common?

Well, the only answers I could come up with are anger, fear – or both.

Could these two emotions, when concentrated, be enough to doom a spirit to an eternity of hell?

I *hope* I'll never personally have to find out the answer to that.

Moving on once more – another completely different kind of location, commonly reported as being haunted, are those secretive, quiet places... you know the ones. The secluded glade in the woodland, those magical hilltop trees, that isolated ancient stone circle – the list goes on.

What of these places? Are the spirits here full of fire and anger? I would suggest they are not. Are they mischievous attention seekers? – Again, no.

So, what sort of spirit inhabits these treasures of nature? Stories over the centuries would have you believe that it's likely to be a hooded figure, silently gliding between the trees – or maybe standing, watching before slowly fading away. These are nature lovers – spirits at peace with the natural world.

There's nothing to fear from these spirits. You'll get a sense of warmth, love, and acceptance, certainly, but you may also have the feeling of being watched – of eyes following your every move.

So, then my thoughts move on.

Does the place make the spirit, or does the spirit make the place?

Or are the two one and the same?

Churches and churchyards are another favourite 'haunted' place – and you'd be forgiven for believing that there's clearly no great mystery to that. Graveyards are full of the dead, right? Of *course*, they are haunted places. But if you're thinking that it's the occupants of the graves that would haunt these peaceful places, then you'd likely be wrong. I mean, why would they haunt it? What could possibly draw a ghost to a graveyard? It's not as if they would have spent much time there in life, is it? No, a ghost wouldn't choose to spend their eternity in a churchyard. There is literally nothing there for them and yet, there are reported ghostly sightings in these places, on occasion, too.

The sighting of a figure, wandering through the grounds and disappearing into the church. Or that apparition, kneeling over a grave, slowly fading out as you approach.

What sort of spirit could be attracted here? Well, there *is* an obvious answer ...maybe too simplistic, but let's follow it up anyway.

Two possible likely candidates for choosing to spend their afterlife in just such a location, are the vicar (or priest, of course) and possibly the groundsman.

These are the people that would have tended these grounds, looked after the church, and comforted its worshipers. Does it not make sense that they would still want to carry out that lifelong devotional duty?

So, would you expect these spirits to be scary? No, I believe not.

I would expect to feel an overwhelming sense of peace, of belonging and maybe, a little pride.

Agree with me or not, that is of course, your prerogative, and besides, differing opinions make the world a more exciting place – but I have laid before you my ideas, my theories that certain types of locations will lead to a certain kind of haunting.

There are of course, exceptions. But you know what they say it's the exception that proves the rule.

I know of one pub – an ancient coaching inn, in this case – that has nothing of jollity and light-hearted mischievousness about it. It is a place of darkness and fear. But then, I believe it has always been that way. Its own history has made it what it is. There are no happy spirits, content to spend their time in that place. The place is dark in nature and spawns' darkness within its ghosts.

So, can the nature of a building be changed by events that have unfolded within it? I believe the answer to be yes. But one dark event could surely not evaporate a hundred years' worth of normal happy life?

I guess – that would depend upon the event!

I remember going to view a little stone cottage once, what seems now like a lifetime ago. 'Rose Cottage.' Such a pretty little place.

Built of large hunks of weathered granite, its small-paned sash windows were all but covered, by the rambling pink rose that had run rampant in its neglect.

I had been given the key by the estate agent and was delighted to have the opportunity for a good look around without someone following my every move –not that it was really large enough to have allowed much following.

Anyway, I let myself in. The stable door opened directly into the little cottage living room. It was quite charming, just as I had expected. But, I don't know.

I looked towards the stairs. Better go up – I guess. But again... I hesitated.

Deep breath, up I went.

Nothing much to see upstairs, just two tiny cottage bedrooms – one, the smaller, would make a great guest bedroom, I mused – but the second... Ah, NO!

The atmosphere here was thick and cloying and crossing that threshold, I had the strong sensation of having to *push* myself into it. Like the stretching of an invisible elastic band or walking against the tide, it felt almost as though it were trying to repel me from the room.

Steeling myself, I made it as far as the window before being treated to a new and unexpected gift, as a sudden wave of nausea and disorientation slammed through me, doubling me over and literally making me gasp.

There was no denying it now. There was something really wrong with that room, and while the going was good, I beat a hasty retreat back down the stairs.

I almost crawled out of that place. I shall never forget it – although it's been over thirty years now since that day. Nowhere else has ever caused me such an instant and violent reaction.

Rose Cottage, so pretty, so reasonable a price – and so empty!

I just knew that I wouldn't be alone in sensing the wrongness of this place, and had to wonder now, if the estate agent's willingness to hand over the key and leave me to it, didn't have more to do with the bad feeling that the place exuded, rather than him being unseasonably busy.

So, one dark event maybe *had* undone a hundred years of normal happy life, for this quaint Cornish homestead. I don't know what that event was, you already know I'm no medium, but it had turned a pretty little Cornish cottage into a dark, haunted place, a place of sickness and dread.

Whatever had happened here, it certainly wasn't good!

So, what does it take for a place to be haunted?

It's not the tales of poltergeists, red-eyed demons, or phantom monks – but be it good, or bad – it just needs that special sense of place.

Chapter 28
# When Investigations Go Wrong

As all Paranormal Investigators will know, oft the most anticipated of investigations, will turn out to be a damp squib. What follows is just one such occasion.

Having crawled our way through the bank holiday traffic jams, we now determinedly shouldered our bags and started up the hellish climb. *(Note to self - oxygen tank advisory for revisit)*. So far, so good – but luck wasn't to be our friend on this occasion.

In the distance, loud music was blaring from the pier across the headland and *worse*, herds of mountain goats were slowly but surely, making their way to the isolated, derelict fort that was to be our destination for the night.

The guys immediately set to, valiantly fighting off the goat invasion *(oh, how I wish I'd filmed that),* leaving us ladies to set up the base room and prepare for the coming night's investigation.

Unfortunately, setting up my gear took far less time than anticipated, because as it turned out, I had managed to leave my entire stock of carefully charged batteries behind, on the hall table by the door! *(Shoot me now)*.

Oh well... Ever the optimist, I've still got maybe an hour maximum of night vision recording, via the camera's internal battery. That has to be better than nothing, hasn't it? But then, joy of joy, down comes the rain – and what rain!

Never mind - it'll keep any unexpected visitors away.

No? You guessed it!

*'Hello...* what are you up to?'

A couple had magically appeared out of the downpour and had proceeded to make themselves a little camp, right in the middle of the fort's central courtyard – and, just to make matters worse, the music from the pleasure pier seemed to be getting louder and louder as the night wore on.

*Wonderful!*

The ongoing battle of paranormal investigator versus goat raged back and forth for another hour or so, before the final and definitive victory – to the goats!

They breached all our defences and swaggered triumphantly into the middle of our ill-fated investigation.

Well, that was it! Time to go home!

A 240 mile round trip that had started with traffic jams on the M5 and ended in victory for goat kind.

Sometimes we learn life lessons under the strangest of circumstances. Today, it was a classic, 'Never mind the ghosts – it's the goats that will get you.'

It's not just our animal friends that can scupper an otherwise epically spooky night, however. Mechanical failure can dog the best of us and literally stop us in our tracks – and it's more than once that our vehicles have let us down.

Worse still, is when you've packed all your equipment, spent the day charging batteries and working out a plan of attack, gathered the team together and set off to our destination – in high spirits and looking forward to a successful investigation.

We're there.

We're on time.

Everything is ready to go.

Just one little, teeny tiny problem. The place is shut and boarded up for the night, and no one is there to let us in.

We have been forgotten. Neglected. Forsaken.

All we can do is peer mournfully through the cobweb covered windows and lament our lost opportunity.

Well – that or shrug it off, as we head for a McDonald's instead!

. . .

So, until now, the downsides of being involved in the paranormal haven't really been that bad - But I can assure you, worse is to come.

Have you ever found yourself in a situation where someone you know well, very well, is suddenly acting like someone completely different?

If a person is affected by spirit and starts taking on a personality, mood or emotion that is not their own, it's called overshadowing. It can be mild, taking the form of a simple lousy attitude or disdain for what's going on – right through to rude or aggressive behaviour.

It happens when someone is unprotected psychically or feeling weak within themselves – and it has happened to me more than once.

One such memorable event occurred while sitting in a fireside seat, at a renowned haunted castle in deepest darkest Cornwall, and I started feeling weird, different – somehow ...*disconnected*.

I knew exactly what it was, but felt quite strong and confident enough within myself, so I decided to let it in, at least a little.

It wasn't long though until the others twigged what was going on. My expression had given me away. It was different, scornful, and disinterested. I felt firmly in control however, and could articulate precisely what was running through my mind – what had been *placed* in my mind.

I told them that it wanted me to call them pathetic and ridiculous. That they had no right to be there – and that they should all get out.

It's an odd feeling, for sure, and unquestionably of great interest to anyone involved within the paranormal field.

On other occasions with me, it has taken the form of strong emotions that simply weren't my own. I have found myself literally in tears, with no clue as to why, and even more bizarre – is to be extremely emotional and start crying for no known reason – whilst laughing my head off about it. The tears were theirs – the laughter, mine.

It is a reasonably common experience, more common than you would think possible – and most people that investigate have come across it at least a few times in their endeavours.

Usually, it will be over fairly quickly – but there are times when it can overflow into your home life and, at worst, has been known to last for weeks.

When overshadowing goes further, though, and edges towards possession, then you really have to be on your guard – and I admit there have been occasions when I have believed myself to be in physical danger, from my teammates.

It's unnerving to find yourself looking through the viewfinder of a night vision camera, at that person you know and love so well, only to find they've taken on the countenance of someone entirely different. Their face, their features, the very way they move – everything is *just not them* anymore – and worse – emanating from them, is a pervading sense of evil – of absolute hate.

Yes, I know that sounds overly dramatic, like something from a movie – but that is how it happened.

So, what did I do?

The only thing I could, given the circumstances. I turned the camera off and insisted we leave, straight away.

I had a fight on my hands that night. The attachment was strong, and the thing within her really hadn't wanted to leave – whining – complaining – trying anything to coax us into staying –into seeing out the night.

I couldn't give in to it, though. We had to get out, and it had to be now.

Under normal circumstances, you would be correct in assuming that the 'take over' would be lessened as soon as you get them away from that room – that space. And for a moment, maybe half a minute or so, it was.

During that brief respite, my friend was back. She looked at me, smiled reassuringly and held out her hand. I had no sooner reached out to grasp the proffered hand though, than it was snatched away – her face changing before me once again, descending once more into whatever hell she had been dragged.

'We need to get her out of here – Now!'

I gestured towards the door. 'Grab the gear, and let's move!'

We cleared our gear out in double quick time, locked up as fast as possible and got ourselves out of there.

I shall never forget, though, looking back towards that place, fumbling frantically as I attempted to re-padlock the gates. As I looked on, a streak of light shot internally across two consecutive ground-floor windows – heading towards the very door through which we had just exited.

Finally, away, that awful influence started to slowly recede, as we silently drove through the night. But oh, it took so long to be totally gone. Many months, in fact – and it changed so much.

With time and distance, my teammate could later articulate the violent thoughts that had been placed inside her head. But it had only served to confirm what I had, deep down, already known.

With time now passed – we began, with some trepidation, to look over some of the footage caught from that night, and what we found was a real eye-opener.

There had been things happening pretty much from the outset – footsteps from above, a weird growling noise, taps and bangs as unseen things had shifted around us – but throughout it all, for the first part of the night at least, we had all remained in high spirits. It was only later, just past midnight, in fact, that things really took a turn for the worse.

The mood of everyone present became sombre and jumpy. We could all sense the coming attack. We'd known what was coming – just not how bad it was going to get.

On review, there had been clear warnings throughout that night. The growl, the bangs – being clearly and loudly told to 'F--- Off!' via an EVP. Two identical recorders were laid side by side when this was caught – yet only one had recorded the voice.

The most significant of all though, was a chilling message that had come through the Spirit Box – unnoticed by any of us at the time.

It was clear. It was ominous.

It was, 'I only need one.'

They were right! They did only need one. If they could get control of just one of us, then maybe, they could take the rest of the team out ...and they had almost succeeded.

## Chapter 29
## Back To The Shadows
My Paranormal Experiences...

It's been too many months now since my last proper investigation. Bad health, bad luck and bad juju have all conspired to keep me from my paranormal pursuits.

Poor health has brought me closer than I would have thought possible to full-on retirement, and I find more and more, that the mind is willing, but the rest of me? The rest of me just wants to go back to bed!

It's a kind of spiritual fugue, a malaise. A disconnection of sorts from the ghostly goings-on around me – and it has been brought on, at least in part, by recent events. Maybe I just lost my nerve? I don't *think* so, but it's true enough that the thrill of the chase has been sadly missing of late.

If I drill right down to it though, one major reason could be that I've pretty much *done* all that I had initially set out to do. I'd wanted to prove the existence of the paranormal – to myself. To be absolutely confident in my own mind, that there is more to this humdrum, day-to-day, *oh, so familiar* existence, that we humans call life.

But I've done that.

I've done it ten times over.

And I now find myself starting to question where I go from here. What possible motive could I have to continue? All that effort, expense – and not to mention, stress! Could it finally be time to call it a day – to hang up the hoody?

I can see no valid reason for me to now shift the goal posts, and attempt instead, to prove the existence of the paranormal to others – to try to change the minds of all those non-believers out there. No, that's one huge uphill struggle that I am just not prepared to put myself through. I simply don't have the appetite for it.

As the months fly by, I find that the prospect of retirement is becoming more and more of an attractive a proposition. But then again, life within the paranormal field is not something that you can so easily walk away from. It's like a compulsion, a craving – and then there's the fact that something always seems to be intervening – calling me back to walk once more in the shadows.

Some of these callings can come about in the strangest of ways too.

Like being invited, out of the blue, to a paranormal

investigation in a building that I had known literally all my life. I had grown up living close to it and passed it when learning to drive. It had always enthralled me – and yet I had never actually been inside.

Do I find it a little weird, that it should be at this late stage in my life that I would finally receive this invite – that I'd get that chance to visit? When it's been over thirty-seven years since I last lived in the area, and it's now a four-hundred-mile round trip, just to get there. Yes, I do – but then, that's life, isn't it, constantly throwing a curveball.

Hampshire, the county of my birth. The place where I first found my love of nature, as I'd endlessly wandered the marshy shallow inlets of Langstone Harbour. I gained my respect for history too, as I'd gazed up at the one remaining tower of Warblington Castle, the reputed home of the ghostly 'White Lady'.

History had seemed to come alive for me when I pictured in my mind's eye, the people named on the old, marbled plaques that adorn the whitewashed walls of the neighbouring St Thomas à Becket Church, and again, while deciphering the faded inscriptions on the gravestones within its ancient Saxon churchyard.

This little part of Hampshire will always hold a fascination for me. It's close to my heart and it calls to me still.

Paranormal-wise, there is just so much for me to

explore. A glut of suitably spooky places that I am just dying to get to visit; Portchester Castle, Racton Ruin and Fort Gilkicker, to name but a few. Number one on that list though, is Fort Widley – and I finally got to check that one off my bucket list, one cold November night.

So, the call – that invite, was to come from someone I'd met quite by chance one day late last summer.

You can tell another paranormal nutter a mile off. I don't know *how* exactly – I mean, yes – it's obvious if they happen to be wearing the obligatory black, pentagram emblazoned hoody – but if not, well, we just seem to gravitate towards each other anyway. Somehow, you just know!

So, there you have it – one ten-minute chat, and now firm Facebook friends and very happy about it, I am too. It's always great to meet a kindred spirit – a like-minded fellow investigator.

Right from the outset though, I knew this event was going to be different. For one thing and for the first time ever, my husband was coming with me.

Now he is not a follower of the paranormal. Oh, he believes in it well enough… I mean, how could he not when he has experienced so much? But he has never felt the need to hunt it out for himself. Preferring, not unreasonably, a nice warm bed to those uncomfortable, cold spooky places to which I am drawn.

He does have a marked interest in all things military

though, so that invite was just too good an opportunity for him to pass up.

That evening, I actually got quite nervous prior to setting off. It had been ages since that last, ill-fated investigation – and having my other half with me too, was definitely going to change the dynamics. I didn't know what to expect – what the night would bring.

Driving up to that splendid arched gateway though, with FORT WIDLEY boldly emblazoned across the top, was exciting. It was a long-held dream for me and a real adventure.

Just one in a string of historic Palmerston Forts that had been constructed on top of Portsdown Hill between 1860 and 1868 – they were designed principally to protect the city of Portsmouth from a landward attack.

Polygonal in design, they are surrounded by deep dry moats, with massive earth-covered banks – that hide a myriad of gun emplacements, armament storage facilities and barracks. All connected by long straight underground tunnels – which radiate from a central spiral stairway that opens onto the parade ground.

The tunnels themselves are brick lined to start, but for the most part, are cut straight into the chalk of the hill. The soft surface of which, malleable and easily marked, is literally covered in carved graffiti. Names, dates, religious symbols – some seemingly dating back to the fort's origins, and a poignant reminder of what has been before.

While the team were starting their investigation, I took the opportunity to head out and about, exploring with the 'old man'.

We pretty much went everywhere. Following our noses – up and down the levels and through enclosed passageways – some of which were so narrow that you had to tuck in your shoulders, in order to pass – and all too many would turn into dead ends, as we poked into every nook and cranny.

The arches beneath the caponiers – the defensive structures designed to house canon for protecting the forts' outer ditches – were to say the least, atmospheric and at times, I had a strong impression that we were being watched off there being a presence lurking within those shadows.

Many times, we found our path blocked by fallen masonry or exceptionally heavy undergrowth and were forced to backtrack. But that was all just part of the fun.

So, satisfied now that we had at least covered the majority of the site, we were heading, once more, down the main tunnel, making our way back to where the team were busy, doing their thing.

I had just passed the magazine – that area designated for the safe storage of shells – when I was startled by a deep voice from just behind me.

Stopping in my tracks, I glanced behind me and then at my husband.

'Did you hear that?'

'What? I didn't hear anything.'

I was disappointed. I could scarce believe that he hadn't heard it too.

The words themselves, had been unintelligible to me. The tunnel system there makes everything echoey and distorted – but I *had* heard something – and it had sounded like a man, murmuring.

At this point in the night, it was time for me to crack on with the investigating. It was what I had come for, after all – and I headed out to join the others, who were by now, attempting table tipping in the rooms underneath the North Caponier …leaving my husband to happily reconnoitre the rest of the fort by himself.

Setting up my sensors, Trifield and Mel Rem, around the room, I had high hopes that some at least, might be triggered. The energy in the fort was ramping up.

That table session was certainly interesting. Even on that rough concrete floor, it had managed to turn several full circles.

The energy was spiky now and the room had an odd feeling. I was aware that several people were present, watching the two of us at the table – but strangely, it felt like there were many more. The room felt somehow *crowded*.

When the session came to an end, the team unexpectedly immediately about turned and headed back to the barracks for a tea break – chatting excitedly as they went.

*Hang on...!* My sensors were still scattered throughout the room!

Now, I am happy to be alone in many places, but this wasn't one of them. It was that feeling of being watched – it was getting to me.

Not wanting to be left behind, I hastily and haphazardly stuffed my equipment into my case – eager to vacate the room and catch up with the others who were already noisily ascending the tunnel. Impatient too, to get out before the one man still present had the chance to vacate the room and leave me *totally* on my own.

Quickly zipping up the case, I grabbed for the handle and scurried off after the others, not sparing so much as a thought as to why *whoever he was*, was still standing there next to the wall, staring seemingly at nothing in particular.

My footsteps rang loud in the tunnel, and I quickly caught the others, content now in their company. I'd not taken more than a few strides further though, when hurried footsteps behind me caused me to stop and glance back.

I couldn't see anything in that impenetrable

blackness, so I directed my light back down the tunnel, fully expecting to see the man hurrying toward us.

But he wasn't there. There was no one.

The tunnel was utterly black and totally empty – and that room beyond...? Well – it would appear that room was empty too!

Where was the man? – *I'd just heard him!*

*Who* was the man?

I really hadn't paid him any great attention – *but oh, how I wish I had.*

I had been aware of his presence as I'd hurried to pack – had been *glad* that he was there, in fact – and that I wouldn't be the last one out of that strange eery place.

My clear recollection is of seeing a tall, slim man – standing upright and staring straight ahead of him, towards the back of the caponier. Thinking back, I have an overall impression of brown, of a sort of sepia colour. Yes, I know it sounds crazy that I didn't take more notice – but my mind was elsewhere – I was in a hurry.

I did see him though or at least, I saw something!

Could it be that I had been the last to leave that room after all?

It would seem so.


After a short break, the last session of the night was to be held in one of the eeriest places *(in my opinion)* in the fort – that central spiral staircase, and the hub for all those radiating tunnels.

The staircase was wide and made of reinforced concrete. Contained within a circular wall and surrounded by an outer circular hallway, off which ran the four spokes of the various tunnels.

The team and I were standing now, spaced out, within that outer circle. In total absolute darkness, we were calling out for something to make its presence known to us – for something to happen.

I was maybe ten feet from the nearest person, yet in that blackness, a deeper black seemed to suddenly lunge towards me, right into my face.

Unnerved, I asked if anyone had moved – but they'd all answered 'no', and the sound of their voices indicated that they were still some ways distant.

Again, the darkness lunged. I could feel the presence of something – it had invaded my space – I could feel its energy, its strength.

This time I turned on my torch, careful to keep the beam pointed downwards. Sure, now that someone was playing tricks on me. But no, everyone was where they had been to start with.

Unsettled now, I tried, once again to chill – to tune into the energies of the place. Within seconds – it happened again. Something was looming over me, and this time it was accompanied by a god-awful low moaning sound, right next to my ear!

That was it for me!

I admit, that freaked me out and I quickly scuttled off to another part of the circle. Nearer to other investigators this time.

Well, the fort hadn't disappointed.

I had heard a disembodied voice, footsteps – as something came towards me repeatedly in the darkness and had heard that dreadful moan. But best of all though was me believing that I hadn't been last out of that room, when it actually turned out that I had.

Well – I was the last *living* person, anyway.

For the second time in my life, I had seen a full apparition and again, it hadn't frightened me. In fact, his presence had actually been a comfort to me. I had been glad that he was there. After all – *I didn't want to be left alone with any potential ghosts now, did I!*

Thinking back to that moment, as I find myself doing more and more these days, I have come to an unexpected realisation.

I now find myself unable to dispel the strange notion that he had intentionally let himself be seen – that he somehow knew I was concerned about being left on my own and had appeared in order to bring me ease of mind. But I'm equally sure there is more to it than just that.

He hadn't been looking at me at all, but had been standing perfectly still, about six feet away from me – just staring at the far side of the room.

As I said previously, the room had felt 'crowded and spiky' throughout that whole session. Could he have been keeping guard for me? – Had he been *protecting me* from the 'others' as I'd hurriedly packed up my gear? Strangely, this is the direction my thoughts always lead me.

I can't help thinking about what might have happened had I realised who and what he was at the time, though. How would I have reacted?

It's a frightening thought for sure.


Funnily enough, just the other day, while I was chatting to my husband about investigating... the subject of Widley had come up, and a strange expression came over his face.

'Actually – I have a confession to make.'

Thinking that he was about to tell me that he had been playing tricks on me that night, I was preparing to get angry. But what he said next though, took the wind right out of my sails.

'When we were in the tunnel, and you asked me if I'd

heard that voice – I know I *said* I didn't hear anything. He looked embarrassed. 'But actually – I did. I heard it too. I just didn't want to have to think about it.'

*Wow!*

Confirmation is always a great thing to get. Even if it does come many months down the line.

# Epilogue

If you've managed to read to this point and haven't yet run for the hills or tossed this into the recycling, then I guess it's probably already too late to save yourself.

Life in the paranormal community can be stressful and hard going. It will take all your spare time, push relationships to breaking point, sap your finances and all for the thrill of the chase.

On the other hand, I can pretty much promise that life will always be *interesting*, that you'll get to meet some of the nicest, most caring people ever, and that you'll make friends for life out of people that you will never actually get to meet in person.

The paranormal community will befriend you, buoy you up and keep you going in the right direction.

Let's be honest though – our chance of obtaining that

rock-solid piece of evidence is almost certainly, just a pipe dream. But isn't that just part of the fun? It's a challenge – something to be overcome.

You want my advice? Go for it! Get yourself out there and find out what it's all about for yourself.

And me...?

Loving all things paranormal as I do – I find, these days, that I love my creature comforts more. Investigations are tending to get easier, shorter and take place earlier in the day.

But that's okay.

I have learnt enough by now to know that it doesn't need to be in the depths of the night for something paranormal to happen. It just needs you, your open-mindedness to spirit, and for that spirit to have a need or desire to make contact.

I will bide my time. Just wait and see what this wonderful paranormal world of ours has in store for me next. After all, I have a date with a certain spirit man in Fort Widley to arrange, don't I? And this time, I'm not going to forego that formal introduction and just leave the room. Oh, no! I want name, rank, and number – thank you kindly, Sir.

So, full-on retirement for me can wait – but there's nothing wrong with a bit of preparation for it. A bit of practice, every now and then, eh?

· · ·

In our pursuit of irrefutable proof of the paranormal, we can plainly never win but – when you get right down to it – it's really all about the chase isn't it?

So, for me – and who knows maybe you too – the search will go on regardless.

## About the Author

As a cynical (getting) oldie, with a lifetime's interest in all things spooky – finally I could resist the call of the dark side no longer and dived, head first, straight down that paranormal rabbit hole.

A crazy decade then ensued. Attempting to see the unseeable, record the inaudible and chasing down those ever elusive leads, whilst getting little to no sleep and living on adrenaline.

I have been lucky enough to have attended hundreds of investigations – experimenting over time with spirit contact, via methods both weird and whacky. Sometimes successfully, and other times... well, not so much. But that's all part of the game. The wonderful game of hide and seek that is investigating the paranormal.

www.ingramcontent.com/pod-product-compliance
Lightning Source LLC
Chambersburg PA
CBHW052113200426
43209CB00057B/1605